Mountains

Visitors to the mountains may stay near the shores of deep, blue lakes. This one is surrounded by peaks and ridges of Glacier National Park, Montana.

Mountains

BY CARROLL LANE FENTON
& MILDRED ADAMS FENTON

ILLUSTRATED WITH PHOTOGRAPHS AND DRAWINGS BY THE AUTHORS

BOOKS FOR LIBRARIES PRESS
FREEPORT, NEW YORK

GB 511
F4

STANDARD BOOK NUMBER:

8369-1129-6

LIBRARY OF CONGRESS CATALOG CARD NUMBER:

70-84305

PRINTED IN THE UNITED STATES OF AMERICA

Contents

CONTENTS

Illustrations

ILLUSTRATIONS

ILLUSTRATIONS

ILLUSTRATIONS

Mountains

CHAPTER I

When We Visit the Mountains

WHEN WHITE MEN came to our country they settled along the Atlantic coast. There they found flat lands, valleys, and low hills that were good for farming, as well as streams on which they could travel or build mills. Settlements spread northward and southward, from Florida to Maine and on to Nova Scotia. Some regions had so many people that farmers felt crowded and wanted to move away.

But when they traveled westward they got into trouble, for mountains were in their way. Those mountains weren't high, but they were very steep and were covered with thick forests. Even sturdy frontiersmen like Daniel Boone found them hard to cross.

But Boone did get across, and so did explorers who were sent out after the Eastern colonies became a new nation. After them came thousands of other people, who wanted to live in what then was the West. They

I

followed roads through deep valleys and over ridges; then they took boats that floated down rivers to Ohio, Indiana, and Kentucky. When the rivers ended, the pioneers used wagons pulled by oxen. Such outfits were heavy, clumsy, and slow, but they did roll on and on across the grassy prairies. "We're through with mountains," people exclaimed. "Now we can go as far as we like—if we don't bog down in mud!"

Yet explorers already had brought word of mountains beyond the prairies and the plains that lay west of them. These mountains were much higher than any ranges in the East, and very much wider. They also were much harder to cross. When people began to go to California and Oregon, some sailed all the way around South America rather than brave those mountains. Others walked or rode, struggling up ranges and letting their wagons down with ropes. Many started too late or took so long on the way that winter overtook them. They had to live in tents or crude cabins, eating wild birds and other game when their food gave out. Those who had bad luck in hunting starved, and others froze when blizzards howled across the peaks.

We may trace these different mountains on the map at the front and back of this book. The Eastern ranges are narrow and long, extending from Alabama to the tip of Quebec. They still divide the coastal regions from the Ohio Valley, as you'll find when you follow the winding roads that have been built across them.

Snowstorms often block those roads, while icy rains that sometimes fall make them dangerous.

A few Western ranges are small and stand alone in the midst of plains. But the really big Western mountains start far from our country, near the tip of South America. They run northward for 12,000 miles, to the southeastern tip of Alaska. Indeed, the highest peak on this continent is Alaska's Mount McKinley. It rises 20,300 feet above the sea, or more than a mile above the highest mountains in Washington and California.

Pictures on the map suggest what some of these ranges look like. In the Eastern mountains you see wide, hilly valleys with farms and winding rivers. You also see ridges, with woods and even fields that go all the way to the top. Western pictures, however, show steep cliffs and mountain peaks that are partly covered with snow. There also are deep, narrow valleys called canyons and others that are filled with lakes. Several of these regions are so beautiful that they have been made into national parks. Here people come for their vacations. They ride, hike, go fishing, or climb. With good roads and trails to help them, they get far more fun out of peaks and valleys than the pioneers did. They even have good times in winter, for trains and trucks bring plenty of food and warm hotels provide shelter when visitors are tired of sports.

Shall we visit some of these Western mountains, to see them for ourselves? We first travel through valleys or across level plains. Here the mountains are so far away that they look almost like clouds along the line where earth and sky seem to meet. As we come closer, the mountains show as a blue, jagged ridge. Notches in the ridge are valleys or canyons; high, pointed places are peaks. Some of these peaks are covered with snow, which glistens when the sun shines on it.

As we ride toward the mountains, the land becomes rougher and rougher. We cross a narrow valley called a gorge, with a river flowing at the bottom. We next climb a gentle hill, but soon come to one that is steep. Other hills are all around us. Many of them really are long ridges made of rocks that seem to be tipped or bent. Since these hills lie near the foot of the mountains, we generally speak of them as foothills.

Now we go around one end of a foothill and into a deep valley. Its sides are so steep we would never try to climb them. At the bottom of the valley is a river— the same one we saw in the gorge. It is not so large here, but it is much faster than it was. Its water swishes around curves, tumbles over falls, and splashes against big stones or boulders. The river seems to run away from the mountains as fast as we are riding toward them.

At last we come to a lake in another valley. Peaks and high ridges surround the lake, whose water looks deep blue or greenish. Near it are groves of pines and other evergreen trees, as well as meadows where bright-colored flowers bloom. Travelers like ourselves camp in one grove, living in trailers, tents, and cabins. Other visitors to the mountains stay in a pleasant log hotel that stands near the lake shore.

Mountains around the valley are high, but roads and trails have been built across them. These roads and trails start in valleys or on meadows and run along the shores of lakes or follow swift, noisy creeks. Then they begin to climb, winding around the sides of mountains and climbing steep slopes in zigzags known as switchbacks. In some places they were made by blasting narrow ledges, or by digging tunnels in cliffs of solid stone. We may take thrilling pictures from such switchbacks, for they make the mountains look much steeper than they really are.

Highways sometimes run along the tops of ranges, turning out to give beautiful views. Others cross the mountains at low places, or passes, and start downhill again. They go down just as crookedly as they come up, winding into valleys and around points, or twisting to and fro in switchbacks.

Let's pause at a pass to look around. We see that each range forms a dome or irregular ridge whose crest becomes a divide. In other words, it separates the water from rain and snow, making it flow in two or more directions. Creeks that go down one side of the divide flow into the valley from which we have come. Creeks that go down the other side flow to a different valley. Sometimes a lake is perched right on the divide. The creek from one end of the lake flows down one side of the range, while the creek that comes from the other end flows down the opposite side.

Some divides run a few miles and stop, but others are connected. A long series of Western ranges form the Continental Divide, which extends from Mexico to the Arctic. Streams on the eastward side of the Continental Divide flow to the Gulf of Mexico, Hudson Bay, or the Arctic Ocean. Streams on the western side flow into the Pacific Ocean.

Trails often climb much higher than roads. They go to windy slopes where trees are small and stunted or are bent and twisted by gales. Then they cross grassy meadows where flowers bloom beside pools of cold water and willows are shorter than the grass. From these meadows the trails go to rocky ridges on which plants nestle in cracks between stones, as if they were trying to find warm corners where the wind does not blow too hard.

There are thousands upon thousands of these rocks— big ones, little ones, and all sizes between. They lie in valleys as well as on mountain tops, and we discover many surprising things when we stop to look at them. Here are shiny, sharp-edged pieces called crystals that formed when molten rock cooled, millions of years ago. There are twisted "ropes" of rock which show that lava flowed like very thick syrup. A slab of sandstone has crisscross ridges that were made when waves rippled over a shallow bay. Hard black shale is filled with fossils, which are petrified remains of things that lived ages ago while the shale was mud. Some fossils are shells and others are seaweeds. Many belong to creatures that were cousins—very distant cousins—of the lobsters and crabs. Their hard shells make the most attractive fossils we can find in any rock.

We also see how the mountains are changing and are being worn away. Near one peak is a huge pile of broken stones, hundreds of feet in height. Every one of those stones broke loose from the mountain, tumbling down slopes and over cliffs until they landed on the pile. Each one made the pile a bit larger and the mountain a bit smaller. In time its top will not rise far above the broken blocks and slabs.

Animals often watch us as we hike along the trail. Those tracks were made by a bear; there he is in that berry patch, sitting as still as a stump until we go away. On a grassy slope gray ground squirrels play; they come close while we eat our lunch and beg for peanuts or crumbs. On one of the high, rocky slopes a marmot sits on a rock and whistles when we come too near. He looks like a big, gray woodchuck, but his whistle is very much louder than the noise a woodchuck can make.

And birds? The mountains have birds of many different kinds. Gray robber jays come to camp for bits of food, but big blue and black jays stay in the woods, where they play and call with harsh voices. Eagles soar

MOUNTAINS

above high ridges, while bluebirds chirp happily as they perch on trees and stones.

They seem to welcome us to the highlands. So let's accept their invitation and set out to discover what mountains really are and how they came into existence.

CHAPTER II

Blister Mountains and What's in Them

WHERE shall we make our first visit to the mountains? We may do so in either the East or the West, and almost anywhere from South America to Alaska. We also may choose snowcapped peaks near the sea, or steep, bare ridges among deserts of the Southwest.

Suppose, however, that we go to northeastern Wyoming, near the little town of Sundance. Here we find a low, dome-shaped mountain that is surrounded by dry, rolling plains. It is so small that some people call it Little Sundance Hill, but ranchmen who saw its pine trees named it Green Mountain.

The story told by this dome began more than 30,000,-000 years ago, when little camels, hornless rhinos, and other queer beasts roamed across the West. In those ancient times Green Mountain did not exist. The only trace of it was a mass, or pocket, of hot rock far down under the ground.

MOUNTAINS

What made the pocket hot? Perhaps part of the earth shrank, squeezing and pushing till its temperature went higher and higher. Perhaps substances such as radium made heat when they turned into other things. This heat made the pocket very warm. It also changed particles of water in the stone, turning them into steam that dissolved tiny grains of minerals. This helped the hot rock to melt and become a lavalike mixture which we call a magma.

The magma was not liquid, like molten iron; the miles of stone which covered it pressed much too hard for that. The most it could do was become rather doughy —in fact, the word magma means "dough." It was just soft enough to move slowly and so to start its long trip toward the surface of the land.

No one is sure how the magma moved, for no one was there to watch it. Some scientists think it was squeezed so hard that it worked upward through weak places in the ground, as mud sometimes works up through cracks in pavement. Others say that steam in the pocket developed so much pressure that the magma was forced upward. Higher and higher it went, pushing through older beds as if it were a huge punch.

A third group of scientists believe that the "dough" melted and dissolved beds of stone above it, turning them into magma, too. If they are right, the hot rock actually ate its way upward toward the plains.

As the magma moved it began to change. The higher

We take a trail that zigzags to a glacier at the foot of a jagged wall. The dark band is once-molten rock that baked beds above and below it into marble.

oads wind through woods, giving views of peaks and hanging valleys that are described in Chapter 10.

Green Mountain is a low dome on the plains of eastern Wyoming. Its core is biscuit-shaped mass of rock that once was hot and doughy.

Beds of rock seem to stand on end in the can-von of the Big Thompson River, in Colorado.

Small dikes of dark, igneous rock cracks in this block of gray gra Such small dikes generally are ca veins

it went the less it was squeezed, for there were not so many rocks above it. Less squeezing meant that the pocket could swell, becoming softer and softer. In time it turned into a balloon-shaped mass that was almost like the molten lava that flows out when volcanoes erupt.

At last the pocket came to a place where it could raise beds of stone instead of going through them. Those beds were limestone and sandstone and were tough as well as hard. In fact, they were so tough that they bent and stretched into a dome-shaped blister that was more than a mile in width. Magma filled this blister and pushed it still higher, while earthquakes shook the plain. They did not stop until the dome and its filling had become Green Mountain.

Rains fell upon the new mountain, and creeks rushed down its sides after every storm. Water seeped down

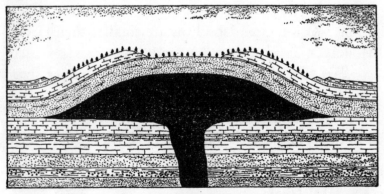

A section through Green Mountain, Wyoming. Hot rock came up through the narrow neck and spread out in a biscuit-shaped mass, bending beds above it. Some of those beds then were worn away.

into cracks and froze, splitting hard stone into pieces which the creeks could wash downhill. As years and ages went by, these processes wore the topmost beds away and cut deep ravines in others. When we look at Green Mountain today we see the "roots" of the worn beds around its edge. Other beds still extend across the dome. They cover a biscuit-shaped core of dark, coarse-grained rock that formed when the magma cooled and became hard again. Dark stone also fills the neck through which the magma came as it filled the dome-shaped blister.

Blister mountains were discovered in southern Utah about 1875. Their scientific name of laccoliths was made from two Greek words that mean "lake" or "pool" and "rock." The man who gave them this name thought that laccoliths were like deep pools of molten rock which pushed the ground upward before they cooled and hardened.

Some of the Utah laccoliths are smaller than Green Mountain, but others are four miles across and as much as 3,000 feet high. Blister mountains of various sizes also are found in Colorado, Montana, Arizona, and other Western states. A few still are covered by beds of bent stone, just as Green Mountain is. Others have been broken by frost and worn by streams till their covers are almost gone.

You can see what such worn laccoliths look like from the picture of Elk Mountain, in southeastern Wyoming.

BLISTER MOUNTAINS AND WHAT'S IN THEM

At its edge are curved ridges, or hogbacks, which are all that remain of the cover. In the center is a cone-shaped peak made of the coarse, grainy rock that formed when the magma hardened. If you climb the mountain, you will find that this hardened core has been worn

Elk Mountain is a worn laccolith, or "blister mountain." Curved ridges are all that remain of the beds that once covered it.

into many steep ridges and cliffs. Indeed, some laccolith covers are so steep that they look like cone-shaped volcanoes. But their coarse-grained rocks and their hogbacks show what they really are.

Let's go now to Rocky Mountain National Park, in northern Colorado. We pass brown and red hogbacks and drive through a narrow canyon where beds of stone seem to stand on end. Then we come to mountains of coarse gray and pinkish granite. Some of these mountains are rounded and are so wide that roads run across them. Others have jagged ridges and steep cliffs which are very hard to climb. The most famous one, Longs Peak, is more than 14,000 feet high.

MOUNTAINS

These high peaks do not look like little Green Mountain, and they formed in a rather different way. Hundreds of millions of years ago land in this part of Colorado began to shift and shrink. The shifting caused earthquakes, but shrinking squeezed beds of stone until they began to bend. At last they formed huge wrinkles of stone that were many miles in length.

But what about the granite? It began as molten rock, much like the magma that filled Green Mountain. It also moved toward the surface, eating, squeezing, or punching its way until it came to the wrinkles. There it spread out and filled the mountains, forming a huge, biscuit-shaped mass that cooled and became coarse granite under the crumpled beds.

If you like, you may call the hardened granite mass a batholith. This name also is made from two Greek words: *lith,* meaning "rock" and *batho,* "deep." We already have found that the magma hardened into granite *deep* down under the wrinkled beds. There it stayed, too, for millions of years until rivers, rains, and frosts wore the rocks above it away.

These mountains are a good-sized batholith, but we may see still larger ones in many parts of the country. Some form mountains in Maine, and others have been worn so much that they now are low hills in the North Woods of Canada. A batholith in Idaho covers 16,000 square miles; you will see part of it if you go to the Sawtooth Mountains. A still bigger batholith forms

Section through a batholith whose crest is worn into pinnacles and peaks. Several dikes cut across beds and two sills spread out between them.

the Coast Ranges in western Canada, for it is seven times larger than the one in Idaho. Magma must have come up many, many times to make that huge mass of rock, which now covers 112,000 square miles.

We also find that many batholiths have had long, complicated stories. The one in Colorado, for example, was worn almost level millions of years ago. Then it sank again and again, and was covered with beds of rock that settled in shallow seas. Long after that the granite bent and heaved upward, forming a new mountain range. You will see other ranges of this kind in the Big Horn and Laramie ranges of Wyoming as well as in the Rockies around Pikes Peak. All these mountains have hogbacks, which are all that is left of bent beds that once covered the hardened magmas.

When you go to Glacier National Park, in Montana, you will see hardened magma that did not form moun-

Hogbacks at the edge of a batholith. Notice that the beds are tilted away from the worn, uplifted mountains.

tains, nor even hills. This magma must have been almost as thin as syrup, and instead of pushing rocks upward, it spread out between beds of stone. There it cooled and hardened into a sill while its heat baked the rocks above and below, turning them into marble. The dark gray sill, between bands of white marble, shows on many high peaks and steep walls.

This magma also worked upward through cracks that cut through older rocks. There it hardened into sheets of stone which stand up or tilt steeply, and therefore are called dikes. When the rocks around them are worn away, dikes stand out as ridges or walls. Some of the most famous dikes in the world can be seen near

Dikes near the Spanish Peaks, in Colorado. They stand out like walls because soft rocks around them have been worn away.

the Spanish Peaks, in southern Colorado. They are as much as 100 feet wide, 50 to 100 feet high, and ten or fifteen miles long. Other dikes are only a few inches wide and are often called veins. Even these small dikes show plainly, especially when they are darker than the rocks on both sides of them.

As we drive through mining towns, we often pass stands where people sell specimens which they call minerals. These minerals are pink, black, white, and several other colors. Since they don't look quite like rocks we wonder just what they are and how they were made.

Let's imagine a pocket of hot, doughy rock, or magma, like the one that made Green Mountain or the Longs Peak batholith. There were many different substances in the magma, just as there are in granite. But things in the magma were melted up together. They were a good deal like the white-hot, molten mixture you may see in a furnace where iron is made from ore.

All these different substances stayed together while the magma was very hot. But at last it began to cool, and the things that were in it separated. They formed grains, or lumps, or flat-sided crystals. Since each one of these was a separate substance, we call them minerals.

When we look at a block of granite near the road, we can easily tell the difference between a mineral and a rock. The whole piece of granite is a rock, formed when the melted pocket hardened. But it is made of thousands of grains, lumps, and crystals, which are minerals. Mineral grains and crystals also form limestone, marble, and other kinds of rock.

Feldspar is the first mineral to harden when molten magma turns into granite. Feldspar may be pink, red, buff, or gray; it looks pearly or satiny but is so hard that a broken piece will scratch your knife. When the mineral breaks it splits into blocks and flat pieces. If you are lucky you also may find separate crystals like those shown in the pictures.

Quartz is the commonest mineral in the world and is found in many other rocks besides granite. It may be white, gray, or pink, but it also may have no color at all. It looks like glass when you break it but is so hard that it will scratch either glass or feldspar. Layers of quartz sometimes fill cracks in rocks, making hard, light-colored veins, but crystals are found in holes or caves. They are pretty things that generally have six sides and sharply pointed ends.

Mica is a shiny mineral that splits into thin, flat

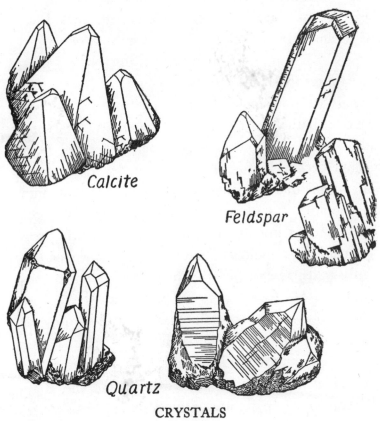

Calcite

Feldspar

Quartz

CRYSTALS

sheets. White mica really is almost as clear as glass; black mica is very dark brown or black. Large pieces of white mica are mined in the Black Hills as well as in Virginia and North Carolina.

Calcite sometimes is called crystallized lime. It is a white or colorless mineral that is softer than glass or steel; you can scratch it with your knife. It forms veins, layers, and "icicles" in caves, as well as clear crystals. These crystals generally are six-sided pyramids, but they will split into flat blocks with smooth sides. Place one of these clear blocks over a line, a cross, or a word. If the block is at least a quarter inch thick it will make these things look as if they were double.

Shall we now look at four kinds of rock that are found in batholiths and blister mountains? The commonest kind, of course, is granite. It formed when magma became hard, deep down under the ground. This means that it cooled very slowly, so that its minerals became crystals or coarse grains. In fact, we sometimes use the name granite for any coarse-looking rock that once was molten. True granites, however, are mostly feldspar and quartz; those that contain almost nothing else are pale gray or pink. But most of the granite you will find contains green or black minerals, too. They make the rock gray. But if the feldspar in it is dark red, the granite looks red or reddish brown.

In New England, North Carolina, and the Black Hills miners often dig useful minerals and gems from a

Mica crystals in pegmatite.

A mass of feldspar (upper right) has broken into blocks with satiny sides.

At the lower right is a group of calcite crystals, sometimes called "dogtooth spar."

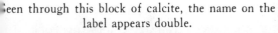

Seen through this block of calcite, the name on the label appears double.

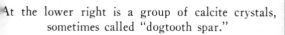

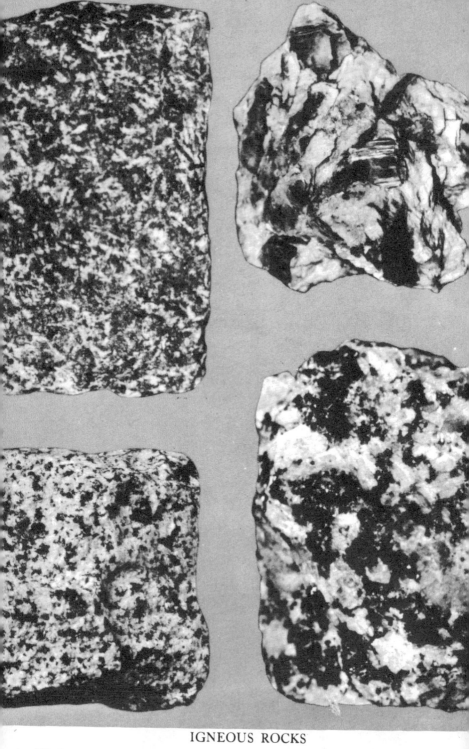

IGNEOUS ROCKS

Diorite
Granodiorite

Pegmatite with mica crystals
Coarse granite

special kind of granite which they call pegmatite. This was the last thing to harden when pockets of melted magma cooled; it was made when steam carried mineral material into cracks in rock that already had hardened. This process made very large crystals. Feldspar may be a foot in length, blocks of mica are six to ten inches wide, and other crystals are as much as forty-two feet long. Pegmatites also contain many crevices and holes, some of which are so large that a man can stand up in them.

Syenite is a rock you may see in the White Mountains of New England and also in some parts of the West. It looks like pink, yellow, or gray granite, but you can tell it because it has almost no quartz and a great deal of feldspar.

Diorite is a coarse-grained, dark gray, or greenish rock that sometimes is called "black granite." It contains a good deal of feldspar, very little quartz, and dark minerals of various kinds. If there are more dark minerals than feldspar, however, we call the rock a gabbro.

You may, of course, find igneous rocks that don't quite fit these definitions. Some cliffs, for example, are made of rock that has almost enough quartz to be called granite. Another kind of rock is almost dark enough to be gabbro but in other respects is like granite, and so is called granodiorite. As you can see from the picture of this rock, it contains a large amount of quartz.

We've said that some igneous rocks have coarse crystals, some have small ones, and some have none at all. Porphyry is any rock that has some large crystals mixed with others that are small. Except for their big crystals, porphyries are like granite, syenite, or other rocks— even the lavas described in Chapter III. In fact, we generally speak of granite porphyry, diorite porphyry, and so on. Such rocks make attractive specimens, especially when the large crystals are bright colored or break so that they show shiny surfaces.

CHAPTER III

Lava Flows and Volcanoes

BLISTER MOUNTAINS are made of stone that cooled and hardened under the ground. In many places, however, magmas rose higher and higher until they came to the surface. There they turned into lava, which is rock that comes out of the earth, or erupts, while it still is hot. Eruptions of lava filled valleys, covered plains, and piled up in plateaus. They also built mountains which are called volcanoes because they resemble a peak called Vulcano, on an island in Italy.

Though volcanoes got their name from Italy, they are common in other parts of the world. We may see huge, old volcanoes in Wyoming or among the Rocky Mountains of Montana and Colorado. Hundreds of smaller ones dot the plains of Idaho, as well as deserts in the Southwest. A long chain of volcanoes forms peaks in the Cascade Mountains, which begin in California and extend into Canada. Some of these peaks are low and small, but others are among the highest and most beautiful mountains in North America.

But remember: lava does not always build volcanoes. We realize that when we visit Lassen Volcanic National Park, near the southern end of the Cascades. The road we choose comes from the north, through a wide, sunny valley where forests of pine trees grow. Soon the bottom of the valley becomes rough, with ridges and hillocks of dark stone. Here molten lava erupted from cracks in the ground, rolling along in hot, fiery streams that burned every living thing in their way. But the flows also cooled very quickly—so quickly that they kept the ridges and ropy twists which show how they rolled down the valley. People in Hawaii call such rock pahoehoe, but we say that it is ropy lava.

At a crossroad a sign directs us to some lava caves. They really are long, dark tunnels which began when specially soft, runny rock gathered inside a lava flow. This soft rock pushed the hardening lava upward; then it flowed away. As it went, it left winding tunnels with curved sides and roofs which break where they are thinnest. Steps have been built in one of these breaks. We go down them, pausing to notice how lava dripped from the cave roof, making stony things that remind us of icicles. The floor of the tunnel is ropy and rough, for the last of the "runny" lava crusted over before it stopped flowing.

From the caves we go to a cliff that is made up of

several lava flows, one on top of another. When these lavas cooled they broke. Cracks started at the surface and went downward, dividing the rock into sections, or columns, that look like logs of wood stood on end. When we look closely, we find that most of the stony "logs" have six sides, though some have only four and others seven or eight.

Another cliff is the edge of just one lava flow. In this one the molten rock was stiff—so stiff that its surface hardened while its under part still was moving. Movement broke the hardened crust into jagged, irregular blocks that tumbled over each other as the lava rolled downhill. When the flow finally came to a stop, its edge formed this rough cliff. We call such flows block lava, though pioneers who had to ride across them often said they were *malpais,* which is Spanish for "bad country."

We discover one fact very quickly as we go from one flow to another. Molten lava alone could not build steep volcanoes, such as Mount Shasta or Mount Hood. Instead, it spread out almost like syrup, flowing in a new direction each time it came out of the ground. Thus it spread out layer upon layer, filling valleys or building plateaus. Much of Yellowstone National Park is a plateau made of very thick lava flows. Still greater flows cover 250,000 square miles in Oregon, Washington, and other parts of the Northwest. In some places the lava is 4,000 feet deep and covers ancient mountains that are half a mile in height. Parts of the Cascades are really the edge of this lava plateau, cut into separate mountains by rivers and glacial ice.

But what if many lava flows came from one hole, or crater? They piled up, one on top of another, building volcanoes that looked like wide, gently sloping domes. Even when they became very high, their sides were not nearly so steep as those of little Green Mountain.

The largest lava dome in the world is Mauna Loa, in Hawaii, which is 200 miles wide and 13,675 feet high. Its sides also slope very gently, as you can see from the drawing that shows its central part. Domes in Lassen National Park are much smaller; one of the best is four miles wide and about 1,600 feet high, which means that its sides are not much steeper than many mountain roads. Another dome, called Mount Harkness, slopes upward from the shore of a pleasant lake.

We soon notice that this volcano contains two distinct parts. The lower one resembles Mauna Loa and is made

The crest of Mauna Loa, in Hawaii, the largest lava dome in the world. Here we see the steepest part of this gently sloping mountain.

of rough, hard lava. Flows took thousands of years to form the broad dome, coming out of a funnel-shaped hole, or crater, located at the top. Then eruptions stopped for a while, and lava hardened in the tube-shaped hole that led upward to the crater. It also bottled up steam and other hot gas that still came from magma under the dome-shaped volcano.

You know what will happen if you bottle up steam in a can or a stopped-up boiler but keep on heating it. The pressure becomes greater and greater, till the steam finally explodes. It bursts the can or cracks the boiler, and may do a lot of damage besides.

The steam in Mount Harkness exploded, too, but it did no real harm. It merely blew hot lava into countless small, bubbly pieces called cinders and shot them out of the crater. The cinders cooled as they went through the air, and some were scattered far away. Others fell back upon the volcano, building a new peak on top of the old crater. Since this peak is cone-shaped and made of cinders, we call it a cinder cone.

There are several cinder cones in Lassen Park, and many in other parts of the West. Some sit on top of dome volcanoes, such as Mount Harkness. Others were built upon high plains covered by lava flows. Most of the cones are dark gray or brown, with funnel-shaped craters and narrow rims. Their sides are so steep that hikers must stop to get their breath long before they reach the top. But if you like you may drive up Mount

Mount Harkness is a lava dome with a cinder cone perched in its crater.

Capulin, which is a cinder cone 1,500 feet high in north-eastern New Mexico. Another cone near Bend, Oregon, also has a steep road winding all the way to its top.

Let's look now at a really steep volcano, such as Mount Rainier or Mount Hood. We think it began as stiff lava that flowed out of a crater on the Cascade plateau. Flow followed flow, building a dome like Mount Harkness—but smaller. Then came steam explosions, which blew out cinders and chunks of lava that piled up in a cone. The explosions were followed by more flows, which covered the broken material, hardened, and so built the cone higher.

This happened again and again, during thousands and even millions of years. One kind of eruption followed the other, piling up layers of cinders or broken blocks and then covering them with flows of lava. Each layer made the mountain larger and higher, till at last

...ria, or bubble-filled lava.

...ll, angular columns of lava
...the Devil's Post Pile, Cali-
...nia. (*National Park Service.*)

...hoehoe, or ropy lava, showing
...w it twisted and wrinkled as
it flowed.

A cinder cone 600 feet high, near Lassen Peak, California. The level ground covered with cinders.

The edge of a block lava flow, showing how the lava broke as it rolled along

it stood thousands of feet above the ridges around it. Mount Hood, for example, is a single cone 11,245 feet high. Mount Shasta is two cones built together; they rise almost two miles above flows and cinder cones near by. Other high peaks of the Cascades were made in this way, and so were such famous volcanoes as Vesuvius in Italy, Mayon in the Philippines, and Fujiyama, the sacred mountain of Japan.

"Well," you may say, "that's interesting—but what about Lassen Peak? It is too big to be a cinder cone, and it doesn't look like a volcano built of cinders and lava. Let's get back to California and find out how it was made!"

Lassen Peak really is two volcanoes, one on top of the other. The first was formed by thin, "runny" lava flows that ran out of a crater. They hardened into dark, glassy rock and piled up in a dome that is five miles long, seven miles wide, and 1,600 feet thick. It contains many, many layers of lava, yet it slopes so gently that we hardly notice it as we drive along the road.

Flows took thousands of years to make this dome— but at last there came a change. A new kind of thick, brownish-pink lava began to come up from the magma under the volcano. This lava was too stiff to run downhill, or even to roll out in block lava flows. Instead, it piled up above the crater in a steep, bulging dome that became 2,500 feet high. This new steep dome, not the old low one, is the real Lassen Peak.

MOUNTAINS

Let's park our car and climb the wide, easy trail that zigzags up the mountain. We soon come to boulders of pinkish rock filled with lumps that are almost purple. They show that the lava became hard long before it got out of the crater. Then the hardened rock was broken to bits, and the pieces were mixed with lighter-colored lava that also became solid stone.

The trail climbs up slopes of broken rock until it comes to cliffs that look like huge, rounded domes and pillars. They show that the stiff lava did not come out in one huge, biscuit-shaped lump. Instead, it formed "plugs" or "spines" that were pushed out of the earth much as tooth paste comes out of a tube. Some plugs were thick and others were thin; some stopped before they got very high, but others formed the topmost peak of the volcano. Most of them cracked and broke as they moved, letting blocks, slabs, and small pebbles roll down the mountain side.

Since Lassen Peak was built by plugs of stiff lava we call it a plug dome. Most plug domes have no craters, but Lassen has a rather large one. We can walk across it safely now, but in 1914 steam exploded from it, blowing out cinders and fine bits called ash. In May 1915 the eruptions became violent, and red-hot lava came from the crater. It ran down the west side of the mountain; on the northeast it mixed with melted snow, forming rivers of mud that ran down valleys and carried enormous boulders to distances of five or six miles.

LAVA FLOWS AND VOLCANOES

Three days later came a blast of hot gas and broken lava which rushed down the bare side of the volcano and toppled over trees on another mountain more than three miles away. After this the eruptions became weaker, and they ended in 1921. But steam still comes from the crater, where our trail winds among blocks of the lava that erupted in 1915.

We look down on a dozen smaller plug domes as we stand on the tip of Lassen Peak. The most famous of these are called the Chaos Crags because their lava broke into a wilderness of jagged towers and blocks. The eruptions that built the Crags ended about two hundred years ago. Then one of the domes was partly destroyed by explosions which sent a huge mass of mud and stones sliding down into a valley and part way up another mountain. This slide is called the Chaos Jumbles; we drove across it on our way to Lassen Peak. We cross it again as we go back to camp, stopping to photograph the cliff that was left when the Jumbles slid away.

The Chaos Crags stopped rising at least two hundred years ago. Lassen Peak had its last big eruption in 1917. Mounts Rainier, Hood, and Shasta have been quiet so long that their tops are covered with snow and layers of blue-green ice.

What do these things mean? They mean that even big volcanoes cannot send out cinders, steam, and hot gases forever. Their lava cools and becomes hard, or

31

the supply gives out. When this happens the fiery mountains "die," which means that they stop erupting. If they are high enough their tops become cold, with snowbanks and glaciers like those we see upon Mount Shasta. Yet the mountains still are volcanoes, for they are made of rocks that were molten as they came up from magmas deep down in the earth.

As we go from one volcano to another we see many different-looking rocks. Some are ordinary lavas, which came out of cracks or craters and quickly hardened into stone. Others are made of lava that was first blown to pieces and then settled in layers or beds. Each one has its own special characteristics, which help us to tell one kind from another and to find out what each kind means.

Basalt is the commonest kind of lava—the one we usually see on plateaus and find in many dome-shaped volcanoes. Many flows of basalt are black or dark gray, but others are dull green or brownish. Broken pieces look dull or velvety, and most of them are so fine-grained that we cannot see their crystals without a strong magnifying glass. Basalt contains very little quartz, but a great deal of lime and iron. The iron causes dark colors, but the lime often forms a white crust on worn, or weathered, blocks of this lava.

Andesite is not so dark as basalt, for it often is gray, pink, or dull red. Most of the rock is fine-grained, but it may contain large crystals of feldspar or dark minerals. Flows of andesite form a large part of Mount Rainier and other high peaks in the Cascades; one flow that came from Mount Shasta ran into the Sacramento River and followed it for fifty miles. Black Butte, near Mount Shasta, is a steep plug dome of pink and gray andesite that contains shiny crystals of the dark mineral called hornblende.

As you probably have guessed, this kind of lava gets its name from the Andes Mountains of South America.

Dacite is a variety of andesite which contains quartz. We already have seen a great deal of dacite, for it forms both parts of Lassen Peak as well as Chaos Crags and other domes near by. The commonest colors are pink, gray, and purplish brown, but the dacite lava that erupted in 1915 is blackish and glassy, with white crystals of feldspar.

Rhyolite is lava that would have been granite if it had hardened deep down underground instead of being erupted. It is gray, pink, reddish, or brown, and it often shows crystals of quartz and feldspar. The name rhyolite comes from a Greek word meaning "to flow," and the rock commonly shows how it flowed while it still was molten.

Volcanic glass, or obsidian, is lava that hardened before its minerals had time to form crystals or grains. Obsidian is shiny and very hard, breaking with sharp edges and points. Black is its commonest color, but red, gray, and brown deposits can be found. There is a high cliff of obsidian in Yellowstone National Park and another in northeastern California.

Pumice is volcanic glass that was filled with bubbles of steam and other gas. These bubbles turned the glassy lava into a frothy-looking rock which is so light that it will float on water. There were cones of pumice near Lassen Peak before the Chaos Crags erupted; you'll find pieces that were blown miles away. A great deal of pumice also was blown out of the old volcano that now contains Crater Lake, in southern Oregon.

Scoria looks like bubbly, cindery slag from a furnace. It really is basalt filled with steam bubbles, but is too coarse to be called pumice. You will find specially fine scoria in some of the ropy lava flows near the Craters of the Moon, which are small volcanoes in Idaho.

When steam explodes it blows lava into millions of pieces. Bits as large as marbles or walnuts are cinders, like those that make up cinder cones. Smaller bits are called ash and volcanic dust; they sometimes shoot out in enormous clouds and are blown many miles by the wind. When cinders, ash, and dust settle they often form beds called tuff. Tuff is a rather soft, fine-grained rock that is not very heavy and smells like clay when it is wet. It may be white, yellow, gray, pink, or brown, and often is mixed with sand or gravel. We find a great deal of tuff among the Rockies, the Cascades, and the Coast Ranges of California, where volcanoes erupted cinders and ash.

LAVA FLOWS AND VOLCANOES

Near cinder cones and lava peaks we may find volcanic bombs. They are lumps of lava that were blown out of craters, just as cinders were. Many bombs were soft at first, but they hardened as they whirled through the air. Such lumps became round, pear-shaped, or twisted, and some of them cracked at the surface when the steam inside swelled.

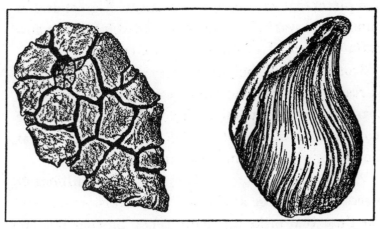

Volcanic bombs. The one at the left hardened and cracked, but the other turned round and round while it still was soft.

Agglomerate is a mixture of cinders, bombs, broken lava, and other bits of stone. This mixture came out of craters or huge cracks; when it fell it settled in layers that hardened and became stone. There are layers of agglomerate in most big volcanoes, and others spread out in valleys near by. The Absaroka Mountains, east of Yellowstone Park, are a thick plateau of agglomerate that has been worn into ridges and peaks.

Would you like one name for all these rocks, as well as those described in Chapter II? Then suppose you call them igneous. This name means "fiery," but we use it for any rock that began as either lava or magma, no matter whether it hardened at the surface or deep down underground.

assen Peak, in California, was formed by "plugs" of lava that were stiff when ney came from the ground. When the lava broke, its pieces piled up in slopes that almost cover the mountain.

Mount Shasta is an old volcano more than 14,000 feet in height. It has two cones and two craters from which lava erupted.

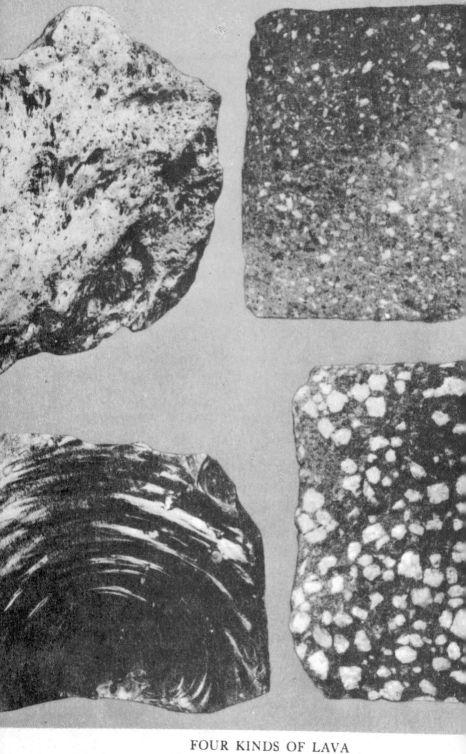

FOUR KINDS OF LAVA

Pumice
Obsidian

Andesite
Dacite porp[l]

CHAPTER IV

Rocks from Ancient Seas

LET'S LEAVE VOLCANOES and lava flows to visit Glacier National Park, in Montana. Here we see jagged ridges and sharp peaks of the northern Rocky Mountains. There are lakes and creeks where we go fishing, and trails on which we hike. They take us from valleys to high slopes where cold winds blow on the sunniest days and flowers bloom beside snowbanks. The trails also climb mountains made of rocks that are green, red, buff, and several other colors.

These rocks make the ridges and peaks look so bright that an explorer who saw them long ago called them the "shining mountains." They look very different from mountains of granite, basalt, and other kinds of stone that once were magma or lava. They tell a different story, too, for rocks in the "shining mountains" settled under an ancient sea.

How ancient? No one knows exactly, but 600 million

37

years is a pretty good guess. North America existed in those days, of course, but it was not like the continent on which we live today. It probably was larger and warmer, and it had several long valleys where the land now is high. When those valleys sank, ocean water filled them and turned them into seas.

The special sea we're talking about was narrow and very long, as you may see from the map in Chapter V. It began at the Arctic Ocean, spreading farther and farther southward across Canada and the United States. At last it met a bay or gulf that came northward from what is now southern California. When the sea and the bay came together, they cut North America in two.

Land west of that old-time sea had hills, mountain ranges, and plains that were almost deserts. In dry weather the wind blew day after day, stirring up clouds of sand and even pebbles, and blowing them out over the water. The wet seasons, however, brought rains as hard as the storms we call cloudbursts. They turned rivers and creeks into floods which washed mud, sand, and gravel downstream.

Even when the rivers were clear they took lime and other minerals from the land. These substances were dissolved in the water, just as salt dissolves when you drop it into a creek or pool. Of course the dissolved minerals went along when the water flowed away.

Do you wonder how we know all this? We know it because streams dropped their loads of rock material, or sediment, when they flowed into the sea. Gravel generally settled first, for it was largest and heaviest. Sand and mud came next, though fine mud sometimes was carried many miles from shore before it went to the bottom. Dissolved minerals settled last of all, for water could hold them more easily than it could hold mud or sand.

As these things settled upon the sea bottom they built up layers and beds. Some were thick and some were thin; some were made of coarse material, while others were fine-grained. Many of them preserved traces of waves, currents, storms, and other happenings. When the beds hardened into stone, these traces became so hard and strong that they have lasted through millions upon millions of years.

Shall we look at some of these old rocks, to find out how they were made? The first one we find is conglomerate, whose name means "something mixed together." Conglomerate began as a mixture of pebbles or even boulders with sand and a small amount of mud. Then the sea water dropped, or deposited, tiny particles of quartz, lime, and an iron mineral that looks like rust. When these minerals hardened, they cemented the mixture into a coarse rock that looks a good deal like old-fashioned plum pudding.

This special bed of "pudding stone" settled in a sea. In some places, however, we may find conglomerates that were made when rivers washed sand, gravel, and

39

mud together and left them in valleys or on low, flat lands that later became hills or mountains. Other beds of conglomerate formed in lakes, where gravel, sand, and mud settled just as they did in the sea.

Beds of sandstone form a cliff near the conglomerate. The dictionary tells us that sand is "tiny grains of broken or worn-down rock." Some of those grains are pink feldspar, but others are dark minerals. Most sand, however, is broken bits of quartz that shine when you hold them in the sunlight.

Every bed of sandstone began as a loose deposit of sand. Perhaps it was clean and white; perhaps it was mixed with mud that colored it gray, brown, red, or blue-green. It was soft at first, of course, for its grains were not fastened together. Then spaces between the grains were partly filled with quartz, lime, or the rusty-looking iron mineral. When these things hardened they cemented the sand into sandstone, just as they fastened pebbles into beds of conglomerate.

Most beds of sandstone formed under a sea, like sandstones in Glacier National Park. Others settled in lakes or on river bottoms, and some even formed on land. They were made where wind piled sand in bare hills called dunes, or spread it over dry lands. When you go to the eastern part of the Uinta Mountains, in Utah, you will see beds of white sandstone that seem to be ancient, hardened dunes.

We know that mud also settled on the bottom of the

ancient sea. Sometimes the mud was olive green; sometimes it was rosy red; sometimes it was almost purple. It settled in layers, just as sand did. The layers were thick when mud was plentiful, but thin when it was scarce. In time they built series of beds, or formations, that were thousands of feet in thickness.

When the beds became thick, they also grew heavy. Thus they squeezed the tiny mud grains together, forming the soft rock called clay. When clay beds were squeezed still more, they turned into shale.

Some shales are soft, rather crumbly rocks; you can cut them with your knife. But most shales in the mountains have been squeezed and cemented until they are hard. They break into flat, sharp-edged pieces which scratch our shoes and cut the hands of people who fall upon them.

Shales in Glacier National Park were cemented and squeezed until they became a special kind of rock known as argillite. Many layers look almost like red or green slate, but others are smooth and rather shiny. Beds of red argillite lie between ledges of white sandstone in several mountains. They form red and white stripes that show plainly on slopes and steep, bare cliffs.

Limestone forms many high ridges and peaks, as well as the sides of some canyons. Pure limestone is white or cream colored, for it contains almost nothing but calcite. Generally, however, this mineral is mixed with other substances that give the rock various colors.

Red clay, for example, makes it dark red; green clay colors it greenish; iron minerals stain it gray, yellow, or brown. Carbon, which is the black material that forms coal, makes many beds of limestone bluish gray or blackish. Other beds are dark inside but rusty brown at the surface, where water has changed their iron minerals.

Dolomite looks so much like limestone that many people never try to tell them apart. Yet this is easy to do if we have some weak acid. Limestone, which contains a great deal of calcite, fizzes when we drop the acid upon it. Dolomite contains a mineral of the same name and does not fizz. It also may be rougher and more grainy than limestone.

Many beds of limestone and dolomite formed when tiny mineral grains settled upon the sea bottom. Other beds are made of broken shells and corals, or of plants related to the seaweeds. These plants grew in threads surrounded by sticky jelly. In some way—no one knows just how—the plants covered their jelly with layers of mineral grains. Thus they actually built rock while they still were alive.

There are thick ledges of plant-made dolomite in Glacier National Park and in the Rockies of Canada. In other places the plants formed ridges, or reefs, like those which corals and other things are building in the sea south of Florida. We can easily tell such reefs from beds in which shells, corals, and limy plants were piled together by waves, forming a hit-and-miss mixture that hardened into stone.

Do you want to know still more about the seas in which many ancient rocks were formed? Then look at a slab of sandstone that lies beside a mountain trail. It is covered with sharp ridges that were made when waves piled up grains of sand under shallow water. When the wind changed, the waves also changed their direction. Soon they built new ridges across the old ones. These sets of ridges, called ripple marks, were preserved when the sand turned to stone.

As waves washed sand to and fro, they piled it in thin layers which lie at different angles, making queer, zig-zag markings on broken beds of rock. Though these layers do not really cross one another they are called cross-bedding. Cross-bedding shows plainly when the layers of sand have different colors, or are worn into low places and ridges as water runs over beds of stone.

But what is this strange rock? It is made of flat pebbles and chips of shale mixed with coarse sand. We think it formed when storm waves swept across a shallow part of the sea. They broke layers of clay to pieces, stirred up beds of sand, and mixed both together. When the mixture finally settled again it became this rock, which some people call conglomerate. A better name is breccia, which means "broken stone."

Have you ever watched a pond dry up? First the water runs off or evaporates, which means that it goes into the air. Then the mud becomes dry and breaks into irregular pieces. Soon it looks like a huge checkerboard divided by hundreds of cracks.

We find beds of argillite or shale that were mudbanks when part of the ancient sea ran dry. At first the mud was sticky and soft—so soft that raindrops made round marks when they fell upon it. Then it began to crack, and the cracks became wider and deeper as the mud dried out. When water covered the banks again, the first thing it did was to fill those cracks with sand or small pebbles.

You can guess what happened after that. The dry, cracked mud hardened into stone, and the crack fillings hardened, too. They show plainly on beds and large slabs, as well as on small pieces that are just the right size for your rock collection.

Sometimes, however, the argillite breaks into little chips. Then the hardened fillings may stick to thicker, stronger layers that cover the mud-cracked bed. When this happens the crack fillings become small ridges that show on the *under* sides of stones.

Early in this chapter we used the name sediment for pebbles, mud, mineral grains, and other things that settle and form beds of rock. Rocks which form in this way therefore are sedimentary. They are very different from the igneous rocks, which are hardened magma or lava.

We know, of course, that sedimentary rocks are found in many, many places besides Glacier National Park.

...aos Crags were built like Lassen Peak. Then one side broke away and slid into a valley, forming the Chaos Jumbles.

...re a mudflow rushed down the slopes of Lassen Peak in 1915. Grass and trees now are growing upon the dried mud.

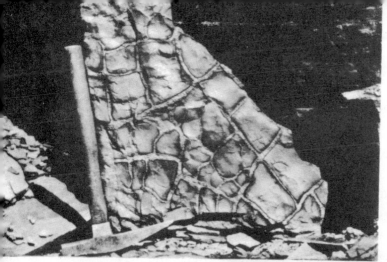

This shale was mud which hardened and cracked when an ancient sea ran dry. When water returned it filled the cracks with sand.

Broken pieces of hardened clay, mixed with sand, form this slab of breccia.

Ripple marks built by waves that shifted as the wind changed, millions of years ago.

ROCKS FROM ANCIENT SEAS

Conglomerate forms hills in New York and ledges in northern Michigan. There is sandstone in deserts and plains and in mountains of the East as well as those near the Pacific coast. Shale, dolomite, and limestone are found under cornfields near the Mississippi River, as well as in hills of Texas and along shores of Lake Michigan. In all these places they look much alike and contain various traces that show where and how they formed.

We also know that sedimentary rocks formed at many different times. Some are much more than 600 million years old. Others settled in shallow seas long after the beds in Glacier Park had hardened into stone. In fact, sedimentary rocks are forming right now. We can watch layers of mud settle in ponds or in quiet bays near the seashore. Corals still build reefs of limestone, while conglomerate is forming where banks of gravel pile up. Waves spread sand out in layers, shifting it to and fro and making ripple marks.

Will these beds ever become mountains? No one knows, for no one can tell what may happen millions of years from now. But we do know that these are sedimentary rocks, and that they are forming just as such rocks formed ages upon ages ago.

CHAPTER V

From Sea Bottom to Peaks

AN ODD-LOOKING BOULDER lies beside a creek among the northern Rocky Mountains. The big stone is made of strong and weak layers that are broken and crumpled. Water has worn the weak layers away, making deep grooves in them. The strong ledges, however, became ridges that wind across the surface.

Suppose we trace this strange boulder's story. We feel sure that it began in a sea, for its layers consist of dolomite and limestone. But why are they crumpled and broken? And how did the boulder get out of the sea and into the Rocky Mountains?

The big stone did not begin as a boulder, of course. It was part of a thick bed of mud that spread over a sea floor for many, many miles. Water in the sea was not very deep, for waves sometimes went all the way to the bottom and bays sometimes dried up, allowing the mud to crack. When western North America moved upward a few hundred feet, the sea bottom became land.

The land did move upward many times, but each time it sank again. Sinking let the sea come back, while rivers brought more sediment that settled in layers and beds. Each bed pressed and squeezed the layers below it, helping them to turn into stone.

At last, however, the country stopped sinking and really began to rise. Upward it heaved and bent—sometimes very slowly, but sometimes so suddenly that earthquakes shook the ground and made waves on what remained of the sea. When the upheavals finally stopped, the old sea bottom was new land. Rocks that had settled under water now formed prairies and hills as well as swampy lowlands.

Forests grew on those hills as well as near the swamps. Some trees looked like palms with round, stubby trunks, but others had leaves like ferns. Still other trees really were palms, which now grow only in warm countries. Such trees mean that snow never fell on the hills and that frost seldom nipped leaves or flowers in those ancient woods.

Queer reptiles climbed among the trees, or soared away on big wings that were covered with skin. Other reptiles, which we call dinosaurs, lived upon the ground. Some of them had webbed feet and flat beaks which resembled those of ducks. A few looked like long-tailed, scaly ostriches; they ran about on their hind legs looking for things to eat. Larger dinosaurs developed horns on their noses and above their eyes as well as bony frills that covered their necks. They were grumpy, bad-tempered creatures that often fought each other with their sharp horns.

For millions of years these reptiles lived in their damp, sleepy woods and swamps. Then things went topsy-turvy again. Swamps turned into prairies, low ridges heaved upward into hills, and earthquakes shook the land. The climate also became cooler and drier as the swamps disappeared.

We call these changes in the earth a revolution, just as we say there's a revolution when human beings change their ways. This special earth revolution was caused when our planet began to shrink and wrinkle, somewhat as an apple does when it withers. Wrinkling produced tremendous force that began to lift rocks, squeeze them, and push them toward the east. Pushed by this force, beds of limestone, shale, and sandstone heaved upward into folds like those you can make in paper. The rock folds, however, were thousands of feet high and many miles in length.

The rocks bent until they finally broke—but they kept on moving upward and eastward over other formations. When the revolution finally ended, beds of ancient limestone, shale, and sandstone formed long mountain ranges which extend from Idaho far northward into Canada. Some of them actually were pushed so far that they

SEDIMENTARY ROCKS

Limestone

Conglomerate

Argillite, a hardened shale

Cross-bedded sandstone

Gray and black shale, bent when
mountains were built

CHANGED, OR METAMORPHIC ROCKS

Slate with crystals of the mineral
called pyrite
Mica schist, made from shale

Banded marble, white and g
color
Gneiss which once was gray g

stood on top of dark rocks that settled in swamps where duck-billed dinosaurs once lived.

Our queerly ridged boulder came from one of these uplifted beds. As hills were pushed upward into mountains, layers in this special bed were squeezed sidewise until they crumpled together. Some of them also were broken into dark and light chips. But the pressure was so great that these chips could not fall apart, as bits fall when you break a stone with a hammer. Instead, the chips were fastened together by other parts of the rock.

Thus the boulder is almost a model that shows how whole mountains were made. We see the mountains themselves when we go to the Rockies of Canada or to Glacier National Park. Ranges near the town of Banff, in Canada, are tipped so much and broken so sharply that they look like huge wedges with jagged tops. In Glacier Park there are peaks whose rocks are crumpled, but in others the beds were pushed so far that they are almost level.

Strangest of all are the ridges and peaks which stand on top of soft, dark beds that formed while dinosaurs were alive. The diagram shows how one of these peaks, called Chief Mountain, was left when the rocks around it were worn away. Another mountain really is a long, jagged ridge where old rocks which are green and bright buff lie on top of younger ones whose color is dull gray. The break between these rocks shows plainly, even when you are miles away.

49

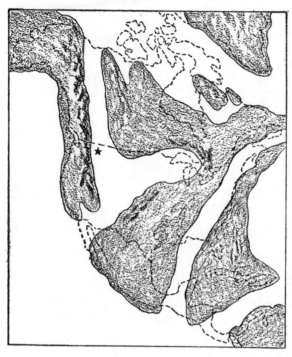

FROM SEA BOT-TOM TO MOUN-TAIN PEAK

This map shows how North America looked about 600 million years ago. Dark parts were land; white ones were seas in which rocks were deposited, as we learned in Chapter IV. The star marks the location of Glacier National Park, Montana.

Other seas spread across the country during later times. Then came the Ages of Dinosaurs, when beds of rock bent upward into hills. The picture at the top of the opposite page is an imaginary slice through some of those hills.

The rocks kept on bending until they broke. Then mountains of old rock were pushed eastward across younger beds, as we see in the second drawing.

Our third imaginary slice shows one of these mountains as it looked when the earth revolution came to an end. Notice that some beds of old rock already had been worn away.

Wear continued for millions of years, until the bent, broken mountain was divided into two. Chief Mountain stands at the front and consists of faulted beds that slipped over each other. The main break, or thrust fault, shows plainly at the mountain's foot.

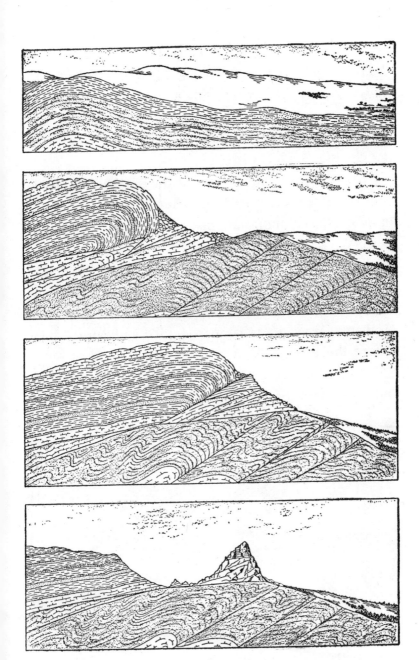

MOUNTAINS

This break has a special name, for it is called a fault. Since it was made when rocks were pushed, or thrust, sidewise we say that it is a thrust fault. If we are in a hurry, we may leave out the second word and just call it a thrust.

Thrust faults show plainly in the northern Rockies, where cliffs are steep and bare. But they also are found in other places, and so are crumpled, or folded, mountains. We see many near the coast of California, where sea beds have been tipped, crumpled, and broken into ranges as much as 3,000 feet high. The Appalachian Mountains, which run in long ridges from Quebec to Alabama, are ranges that were folded and faulted long before the Rockies even became hills.

Rocks broke or bent when mountains were folded, but they often did more than that. Look at a piece of

Summit Mountain, near the southern border of Glacier National Park, Montana. Here the thrust fault is almost horizontal, and most of the crumpled old rocks above it have been worn away.

52

sandy rock from a mountain where beds were squeezed a great deal. You will find that the sand grains were covered with coats of quartz that made them almost like tiny crystals. These coats fasten the grains together very tightly in a hard, glassy rock whose proper name is quartzite.

When shale was folded and compressed, it became slate. Pressure turned old minerals into new ones whose grains were thin and flat. It also arranged the grains in layers, which generally cut across the beds. Slate is split into these layers, which often show stripes or bands that represent the original beds.

Shale sometimes was squeezed and crumpled so much that it turned into schist. This rock generally looks shiny or satiny, for it contains tiny flakes of mica that glisten brightly. They also allow it to split into thin layers. Most of these layers are irregular, while some are so much crumpled that they remind us of paper after it has been crushed into a ball.

Some limestones changed very little when mountains were made. Others turned into marble, for their grains of calcite became shiny blocks that are almost like crystals. Dark layers were turned into cloudy bands that show plainly when the marble is polished.

Dolomite sometimes became marble, too. Its crystalline blocks may be smaller than those of limestone marble, and the whole rock may be a bit darker and harder. Of course, it does not bubble when acid is dropped upon it.

Igneous rocks also were squeezed and changed when many mountains were built. Granite, for example, was turned into gneiss, whose name is pronounced "nice." It contains crystals or blocks of quartz and feldspar, as well as flakes of mica and grains of other minerals. All are arranged in irregular layers that make the rock look banded or striped.

When gneiss was changed still more, it developed new minerals and many small flakes of mica arranged in thin layers. In other words, it turned into schist, which also is made from shale.

Can we tell the two kinds of schist apart? Not always, for the sort made from granite may look like the kind that once was shale. To make things more puzzling, you may even find gneiss that was made from conglomerate instead of granite. Unless it still contains a few pebbles, there is no way to tell just how it began.

But that is not all. Heat and steam from magmas change rocks, even though they are not folded. A dark, "runny" magma baked beds of dolomite in Glacier National Park, turning them into white marble. Batholiths have turned rocks into gneiss and schist in many places. The great marble deposits of New England were made when magmas brought steam that worked through folded formations of limestone.

Yes, rocks have changed in various ways, and we

can't always tell just what happened to some special bed. But don't let such puzzles bother you too much. Learn to know the important kinds of changed or metamorphic rocks when you find them and tell how they formed if you can. If you can't, just remember that the experts don't always know whether heat, steam, pressure, or all three produced some kinds of stone.

CHAPTER VI

Living Things of Long Ago

SUPPOSE we look at several pieces of stone from mountains whose rocks formed in the sea and then were pushed upward. Some slabs are just limestone and hard shale; two or three rough blocks are sandstone. Other pieces, however, contain fossils. They are remains of things that lived long ago and were buried in the rock.

Some of these fossils are petrified snail shells, or shells that have "turned to stone." Others are corals that look like honeycombs or tiny horns and queer jointed animals that remind us of crabs. Several slabs are covered with shells which are round, oval, or almost flat. When we examine one closely, we see that it has two parts, or valves, which look like the lamps that were used in ancient Greece and Rome.

Millions upon millions of years ago this lamp shell lived on a mudbank under a shallow sea. It never crawled like a clam or snail, for it was fastened down by a long, tough stalk that burrowed into the mud. When it was hungry it opened its two valves, swallowing tiny animals and plants that drifted in the water. If anything disturbed the lamp shell, its stalk shortened and pulled the whole animal down against the mud.

The odd creature lived in this way for several years, building its shell larger and thicker. But at last it became so old that it died. Its stalk and soft body decayed, but the shell lay upon the sea bottom until it was covered by mud. Then more and more mud settled, forming beds which hardened into stone that finally became mountains.

While all this was going on, something else happened. Water moved through tiny holes in the rock and began to dissolve particles from the dead lamp shell. But when the water took a bit of shell away, it left a mineral grain that had just the same size and shape. This happened thousands or millions of times, until the whole shell was petrified.

Would you like to find some fossils for yourself, instead of just looking at those which someone else has discovered? Then suppose we go to a high ridge in the Rockies, near the little railroad town of Field, British Columbia. Since the ridge is in a national park, we shall need a permit to collect. We also take hammers, chisels, and bundles of paper in which to wrap our specimens.

We set out on a bright, sunny morning. Our trail

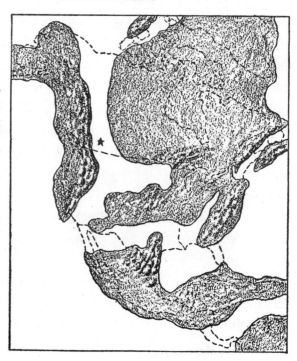

North America as it looked about 500 million years ago. The star marks the fossil quarry near Field, British Columbia.

starts in a valley near a cabin camp and then switchbacks up a steep slope. Soon it crosses a low ridge, or pass, and follows the bare side of the ridge where we look across range after range of mountains and down upon an emerald-green lake. Our map shows that we are a half mile above its rippling water!

Where dark ledges of rock and talus join, we come to the fossil beds. They were discovered many years ago by a scientist from Washington, D.C. The specimens were so good that he brought tools, pitched his camp near the ridge, and opened a small quarry. There he dug and blasted summer after summer, collecting more than 35,000 specimens which he sent to the United States National Museum. When he finished, several other collectors came to the quarry for fossils which he left behind.

Plenty still remain for us, as we find when we look among pieces of shale lying near the quarry. Our first find is a slab of oval lamp shells; then come some feathery seaweeds. They are not really petrified, but are thin films of shiny black stuff, or carbon, that was left when the seaweeds decayed. Rough, vase-shaped things are fossil sponges, while specimens that look like flat pods really are shells of animals that were distant cousins of shrimps. Those jointed creatures with long "feelers" are trilobites—old-time relatives of the king crabs that live near Atlantic shores today. Several slabs show molds, or impressions, of trilobites in hard rock. We decide that they are fossils, too, even though the shells have disappeared.

How did these different creatures live? The best way to answer that question is to take an imaginary trip to this region before they became fossils.

Are you ready? Then down we go to the flat, muddy bottom of a shallow sea. Greenish light flickers down through the water, falling on clumps of feathery green seaweeds that wave to and fro. Other seaweeds are olive brown, with thick stalks and broad things that look like leaves. Sponges grow in little clumps. They have yellow, pink, or orange flesh, and look very different from the sponges we sometimes buy in stores.

Small lamp shells are almost everywhere. Some are fastened to seaweeds; others have tough stalks of their own which reach down into the mud. They close when we touch them, or when trilobites come near. The largest of these trilobites swim or crawl over the mud, tapping here and there with their feelers, and staring with their goggle eyes. Tiny kinds that are blind burrow among rubbish on the bottom, where they find dead things to eat. Sight would be useless to animals with their digging, grubbing way of life.

Here comes a whole school of shrimplike creatures which swim backward by flipping their tails under their pale green bodies. They move much faster than their relatives with the pod-shaped shells. The latter keep close to the bottom, making bouncing movements when they go from place to place.

We might keep on and on with our imaginary trip, for many strange animals lived in the ancient sea. But our watches say it is half-past three: time to pack our specimens and start back to camp. We select the best fossils, wrap them in paper, and put them into our knapsacks. Broken pieces are left behind, and so are several heavy slabs that contain only a few fossils. The trail down the ridge is long and steep, and loads will seem as heavy as lead before we get to the bottom. Let's not make them heavier by taking specimens that are mostly stone!

Shrimps and trilobites lived in the sea, and so did horn-shaped petrified corals such as those found near Banff, in Alberta, where many people go for their mountain vacations. Other fossils, however, lived on land. We described some of them in Chapter V, and find others when we go to the Dinosaur National Monument, in Utah.

About 140 million years ago the country that now is eastern Utah was low, moist land. It was covered with forests of trees, ferns, and the tall, stiff plants called horsetails. Rivers flowed through these forests, carrying loads of sand and clay which they dropped when they flowed into big, swampy lakes.

This was long before reptiles with beaks lived in forests that now are covered by the northern Rockies. But there were dinosaurs in ancient Utah, too, and some kinds were much bigger than any that lived during later times. A few were ninety to one hundred and twenty feet long, with rounded bodies and thick legs, but long, slender necks and tails. They weighed forty or fifty tons, and were so heavy that they had to stay in deep water, where they could partly float. They took mud baths, waded from one pool to another, and ate bushels of juicy plants at each meal. They did not chew their food, since their teeth were not good for chewing. Instead, they swallowed irregular stones, which rolled to and fro in their stomachs and so ground up tough leaves or stems.

Other wading dinosaurs were only eighteen feet long and five or six feet high at the shoulder. They could go into shallow water, but they kept a close watch for hungry reptiles that fed on meat instead of plants. Those meat-eaters had hooked claws and big mouths with many long, sharp teeth. They walked on their hind legs, using their long tails to balance their thick bodies.

Some of these reptiles were caught in quicksands and others were drowned by floods. Rivers washed the dead bodies away, piling them up in quiet bays where they soon decayed. Then sand was piled over their bones, which slowly petrified while the sand hardened into stone.

Their bones lay for millions of years, while shale and other rocks settled. Then the land began to bend upward into ranges of dome-shaped mountains. Higher and higher they went, while the beds were tilted more and more steeply. At last the old lake bottom almost stood on edge.

A guide takes us to the main deposit of dinosaur bones, which now is a ridge of sandstone partly covered with gray and purplish shale. In one place we find eight or ten ribs, still fastened to sections of the backbone. Near them is a big leg bone, taller than a man. That long series of bones once was a neck, which some old dinosaur stretched upward when he was looking for enemies. Polished rocks are "gizzard stones" with which he ground food. They remind us of the grinding stones in a chicken's stomach, or gizzard.

We also look at white, buff, and red rocks that formed in seas and on sandy shores before the dinosaurs lived here. Then the guide brings us back past a quarry where museums got petrified skeletons of these ancient reptiles. "The bone beds were discovered in 1909," he tells us. "Between 1909 and 1923 three museums dug 900,000 pounds of bones from this quarry and shipped them as far away as Pittsburgh and Washington, D.C. There the bones were cleaned, mended, and put together for people to see. So the dinosaurs' adventures did not end when they died, nor when the beds of sandstone and other rocks were bent and tilted into mountains."

We've found petrified sea creatures and dinosaur bones; let's now look for trees that grew upon ancient lands. We find some near the dinosaur beds in Utah, but the fossil logs have been broken so badly that only small pieces remain. They aren't nearly so large as some we shall see at the Petrified Forest near Calistoga, California.

There really are two petrified forests, one above the other. They grew about 10,000,000 years ago, when northern California was warmer and drier than it is today. It was much less peaceful, for earthquakes shook the ground and volcanoes erupted molten lava as well as clouds of ash. Sometimes the ash came out in hot blasts like one that rushed down Mount Lassen and knocked down trees three miles away. At other times it settled in beds, covering fallen logs and even dead, dry leaves.

We find the logs as we walk along a wide, easy trail. Some lie on the surface of the ground; others have been dug out; some still are partly covered by beds of hardened ash, or tuff. Every one is a redwood, almost exactly like redwoods that still grow in valleys a few miles away. If we search carefully, however, we may find leaves of oaks, myrtles, and a few other trees.

One grove of redwoods grew and died—perhaps it was blown down by a blast from the St. Helena volcano only four miles away. Then the logs were covered with ash that piled up layer by layer until it was twenty feet thick. Then another forest grew and died, and was covered with still more ash. One of these trees is eight feet thick; the part we can see is 126 feet long, and another 100 feet are buried in the mountain side. Another measures twelve feet in thickness, but is not nearly so long.

The California redwoods fell to the ground before they were covered with beds of volcanic ash. But we'll see ancient trees that still stand upright when we climb to Specimen Ridge, in Yellowstone National Park.

Specimen Ridge is not quite a mountain, yet it is too high to be a hill. It really is the edge of a plateau that was built when volcanoes threw out ash, pebbles, and large rocks that became agglomerate. The agglomerate

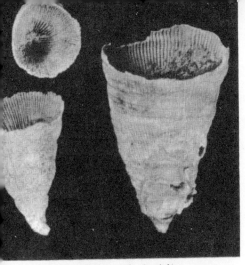

p corals, taken from a bed of limestone. Others are found in shale.

A slab covered with wide lamp shells. They are not so old as those found near Field, British Columbia.

ctions of backbone in sandstone of Dinosaur National Monument, Utah. Great numbers of petrified bones have been quarried from this special deposit.

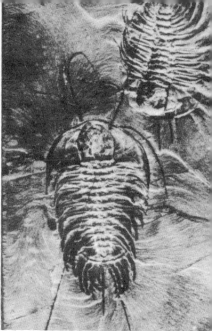

Two trilobites on a slab of black shale found near Field, British Columbia

At left petrified redwoods dug from beds of volcanic ash. Near Calistoga, California.

The authors measure a slab of mud-cracked argillite on a mountain in Glacier National Park, Montana.

weathered into rich soil, where forests of redwoods grew along with other trees. Then the volcanoes erupted again, sending out ashes and lava boulders that fell upon the forests. They broke branches, killed seedlings, and started fires; they half buried living trees and covered others that had fallen.

This happened again and again, for you can find remains of at least ten buried forests as you climb Specimen Ridge. At the top are those whose trees still are upright. Erosion has worn the agglomerate away, so that stumps and tall trunks stand near the rim of a cliff. We measure several trunks that are more than two feet thick while one redwood stump is more than six feet.

These old, petrified redwoods still are large trees. No wonder they stood up through eruptions which covered them with broken rock and built a high plateau!

CHAPTER VII

How Mountains Grow Old

HIKING ALONG A TRAIL, we come to a slope of slide rock. It is a huge pile of blocks, slabs, and small chips that have come loose from a mountain and have tumbled into the valley. At the foot of the slope a creek splashes over the stones and rolls some of them downstream. Farther on it flows through a deep, narrow valley which we call a canyon.

The slide rock, creek, and canyon show us that mountains break to pieces and are worn away. They also tell how ranges and peaks grow old, till they finally turn into low ridges or separate hills.

What makes mountains break to pieces? We can answer this question by climbing to a high, bare cliff. The sun shines upon it all day, making the rocks very hot. At night, however, they cool quickly as the air becomes chilly. These changes make grains and crystals pull apart or crack, just as hot glass cracks when you cool it suddenly. When hundreds or thousands of grains split, they let chips and curved slabs break loose from the rocks.

While the cliff is being heated and cooled, rain water falls upon it and soaks into holes and cracks. When it gets there, it dissolves some minerals and changes others. Most of the changed minerals are not so hard as the old ones and not nearly so strong. They let pebbles fall out of conglomerate; they let sandstone crumble into sand, and they make shiny schist so soft that it finally turns into clay. They also turn granite into a loose mixture of feldspar crystals, quartz grains, and flakes of mica. Men who build roads or trails through the mountains cut into this "rotten" granite with picks or dig it away with shovels.

Sunshine, cold, and rain are parts of the weather; when they break rocks to pieces we say that they cause weathering. We may see weathered rocks almost anywhere, but we specially notice hard parts that are left after crystals or grains break loose and are carried away. Such "left-over" rock often forms ridges and towers on the tops and sides of mountains.

Some weathered granites do not crumble, but break into curved "peels" that remind us of layers in an onion. We see shells such as these in Yosemite National Park; when they break loose and fall into valleys, they leave smooth, dome-shaped mountains. Stone Mountain, in Georgia, is a well-known mountain of this kind, and there are others in North Carolina and New York. No one knows just why the rocks in these mountains break into "peels" before they crumble.

Water changes minerals and makes them soft, but it does another important job of weathering by freezing after it soaks into cracks. In the winter it stays hard for months at a time, but during the spring, the fall, and summer "cold snaps," water freezes at night and melts the next day. Then it may freeze again as soon as the sun goes down. This goes on day after day, as long as sunshine is hot and nights become freezing cold.

Such freezing is important because water becomes larger when it turns into ice. As it swells, it soon begins to push against the sides of every crack. The colder it gets, the more the ice pushes. In really cold weather it presses with a force that amounts to several thousand pounds on every square inch of rock. That is enough to make narrow cracks open into wide ones, to move thick blocks, and to split stones into jagged pieces. It covers mountains like Pikes Peak with broken stones, turns ridges into piles of slabs, and pries blocks of rock loose from cliffs. We must be careful when we climb over such blocks, for many of them are ready to tumble down the mountain side.

They are ready to fall, and weathering helps them go. They slide after rains, when ledges get wet, or they are pushed by snow. Many tip and fall at night as the air grows cold. Small pieces break or move, letting big

Huge, curved "peels" of granite have broken and fallen from this cliff in Yosemite National Park, California. Peels also shaped the dome at the top of the cliff.

Weathered, crumbling granite in the desert mountains of Joshua Tree National Monument, California. Notice how rough the rocks look.

Tilted Mountain, in Banff Park, Canada. These beds were tipped, broken, and pushed upward when the northern Rockies were built.

A boulder showing crumpled, broken layers of limestone and dolomite. It almost a model of a folded mountain.

ones tilt. They teeter for a moment and then go, bouncing from one ledge to another. Sometimes they break into pieces that keep on falling and bouncing. Often they knock other stones loose, and the whole lot comes tumbling down onto the pile of slide rock, which we also call talus.

Suppose we now look at the creek which flows past the talus slope. At first it is only a trickle, but water from rain and melting snow make it larger and larger. It splashes from ledge to ledge, whirls around broken rocks, and washes sand downstream.

Sand helps the creek in its job of wearing mountains away. The water drives sharp grains against ledges and stones, or whirls them into cracks. In this way it scrapes bits from hard rock, just as sandpaper scrapes bits from a block of wood. The creek also loosens blocks of stone, which then drop into the water. The sand rubs against them, too, wearing them down into boulders that become smaller every year.

In one place the creek flows so fast that it rolls pebbles along the bottom. Then it comes to a spot where the water eddies, or whirls about. Round and round the pebbles go, too, wearing potholes in the rock. When the water is low we can look into these holes and see the pebbles that make them. We also can find potholes that were left high and dry as the creek cut its channel deeper. Sometimes the dry holes are so close together that they make ledges look like huge honeycombs.

Next the creek comes to a place where cracks cut through the rock. They give sand a good chance to wear, and they divide the rock into blocks that break loose easily. With such help the creek has worn a gorge, or canyon, whose sides are as steep as walls. In some places they even overhang.

As we go downstream we find that the creek has made its canyon wider and wider. Soon it becomes an ordinary valley, whose sides are covered with woods and grass. At last the valley has been worn so wide that the creek wanders to and fro, across bottom lands that are almost flat. But even here the creek washes soil away from its banks, rolls gravel downstream, and wears large stones down into pebbles. The stream still is doing its best to wear the mountains away.

As mountains break to pieces and are worn down, they also become old. Suppose, for example, that we have a young range whose rocks have been bent and broken as they were pushed upward. They may contain dikes and sills, too, or even great masses of granite like those we described in Chapter II.

At first the mountains are high, with domes and cliffs made by faults. Those cliffs soon begin to crumble, forming talus slopes while streams wear gullies and ravines. Still, neither weathering nor water has had time to change the uplifted land much, so we say that the mountains are young.

Thousands of years now go by. Weathering makes

rocks break and crumble, while streams wash broken stone away. They wear gorges or canyons where the rocks are hard, and scour out wide valleys where formations are soft or weak. These valleys divide folds and domes into ridges, or leave parts of them in steep peaks that are thousands of feet in height. Thus the mountains become rough and "middle-aged," or mature.

After the highland reaches this stage it begins to grow old. Cliffs crumble until they are gentle slopes covered with broken talus. Streams cut their valleys wider and wider, and wear ridges and peaks into hills. At last the range becomes only a rolling plain, where rivers flow lazily. Only a few dome-shaped mountains remain where rocks are so hard and strong that they wear very, very slowly.

When we visit the West we see many ranges whose mountains have just become mature. We can tell them by their peaks and steep ridges and by their narrow canyons. They are much more rugged than mountains which "grew up" long ago and are now becoming old.

There are middle-aged ranges in the West; you'll cross their rounded ridges and see their blunt peaks if you drive through northwestern Colorado. But they aren't so common as they are in the East, where mountains were built millions of years before those in Colorado began. The Adirondacks of New York, the Great Smokies, and the Blue Ridge all are famous mountains that have been worn and weathered for ages. They remind us of some middle-aged people who are plump, have round shoulders, and never stand up straight.

Other ranges in the East became old long ago. Look at hills in Maine and the North Woods, or rolling farms in western New Jersey. They are mountains that have been worn down again and again, till only their roots are left. These roots are broken, crumpled beds, or slopes of coarse-grained, granite-like rocks that once were batholiths.

CHAPTER VIII

From Ridges to Island Peaks

SUPPOSE we leave old mountains of the East and drive along U.S. Highway 97, in southern Oregon. In the west we can see the Cascades, but our road runs through a flat valley that is partly covered by Upper Klamath Lake. On the east are cliffs 800 to 1,100 feet high. They run beside the road for miles, like steeply slanting walls.

These walls show us how mountains of another kind are made, and what they look like when they are very young. Only a few thousand years have passed since this whole region was one long, flat valley, twenty to thirty miles in width. Then the land began to shift, rising and breaking into long blocks whose western sides tipped upward. Up they went again and again, causing sharp earthquakes and making cliffs. Breaks at the foot of the cliffs are faults, even though they are not like the faults we saw in the Northern Rockies.

73

The tilted blocks near Upper Klamath Lake are not mountains, for they have not risen far enough. Other blocks, however, have tilted much more and have gone a great deal higher. They form ranges that are many miles in length, with peaks, valleys, and ridges. Some of them also are very high—higher than the Rockies of Colorado or the volcanoes in the Cascades.

Most block mountains lie in a part of the country which is known as the Great Basin. Early explorers called it the Great American Desert, for almost no rain falls upon it during the long, hot summer. The mountains look dry and scorched; some have forests of cactus plants instead of trees. Little rivers disappear when they get to the valleys, or flow into shallow lakes that dry up in June or July. Then winds howl across the dry lake bottoms, blowing white dust away in clouds or taking it up in whirlwinds. Whirlwinds also break off dead tumbleweeds or bushes and whirl them round and round through the air.

Three questions come to our minds as we travel across the Great Basin. First, what makes it so dry and so hot? Second, why do its mountains look different from those in other regions? Third, how have they changed and grown old in a country where streams disappear instead of flowing to the ocean?

Fossils show that the Great Basin once had a moist climate, with forests of evergreen trees. Then the land broke into blocks, like those near Upper Klamath Lake.

The block farthest west was extra large—a batholith of gray granite 400 miles long and 70 miles wide, whose crumpled cover was almost worn away. This block tipped upward, lay quiet, and then tipped again, rising about two miles. Thus it formed the Sierra Nevada, which is one of the greatest fault blocks in the world.

While this was happening, lava flows and volcanoes built the Cascades. In time the two mountain systems came together a few miles south of Lassen Peak. Thus they formed a wall that runs from southern California to Canada. Though many tilted rocks and volcanoes lie east of this wall, none is so wide, so long, or so high as the Sierra-Cascade ranges.

The two diagrams on page 76 show moist winds that blow from the Pacific; they go over the high mountains, are chilled, and drop their moisture as rain or snow upon the western slopes. Little water remains in the air that goes on over the Great Basin. That little does not fall in the valleys, but on the highest ridges of the tilted blocks. The rest of the basin is left as a dry, sun-baked desert.

But there's more to the process than that. Air drifts upward over the mountain wall; as it goes higher and higher, it becomes "thin," or expands. But as soon as it crosses the wall it comes down and is packed together again, or compressed. Compression raises its temperature. By the time air has come down two miles or more it blows in scorching winds that sweep across the deserts.

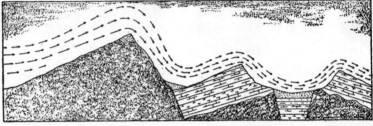

Why the Great Basin is dry and hot. In the upper diagram we see clouds rising as they cross the Sierra Nevada. So much of their moisture falls as rain or snow that only a little is left in the air when it gets to the Basin. Arrows in the lower drawing show how air expands above very high mountains, but is compressed as it goes down into valleys. Compression raises its temperature, making it very warm.

In Death Valley, the hottest part of the basin, thermometers sometimes rise to 132 degrees. Temperatures of 100 degrees in April are ordinary spring weather!

This shows why the Great Basin is a desert, even though parts of it are not far from the sea. Now let's find out why the mountains look different from those in other regions.

We already have given one reason: the fact that these ranges are dry. Few trees can grow on them, and they may not even have grass. Only the highest ones have snow in summer, and their streams run dry soon after

Potholes and pebbles that dug them
Glacier National Park.

Talus cones at the foot of a cliff i
the Canadian Rockies.

Worn boulders lie in the bed of this
mountain stream.

These cliffs beside Upper Klamath Lake were formed when blocks of rock broke and tilted.

Slickens made when rock was polished and scratched as it moved along a fault.

Middle-aged block mountains near Great Salt Lake show steeply tilted beds.

the few rains that do manage to fall. While they do run they are very swift, cutting narrow canyons instead of ordinary valleys.

The mountains also are different because they are tilted blocks. One side of each block slopes rather gently, but the one that broke and tipped upward often is very steep. The faulted side, or scarp, of the Sierra Nevada is a series of ridges and cliffs almost two miles high. Many smaller blocks are just as steep, though they do not rise so far.

To answer our third question we must trace the whole story of block mountains from youth to old age. We already have seen the first part of this story, for those ridges in Oregon are young. Indeed, they are so young that streams have not had time to wear them into cross ridges. In some places the cliffs still look smooth or show how they were polished and scraped as blocks of land tipped upward. Such polished places, called slickens, will disappear very quickly when the cliffs are worn away.

Let's visit now a part of the Great Basin that lies in northeastern Utah. It, too, is a region of steep, ridge-like ranges surrounded by flat plains. Our guidebook says those plains are the bottom of an ancient lake that formed during the Ice Age. It was much larger than Great Salt Lake is today and very much deeper. We can see where its waves piled up beaches and wore cliffs high upon the mountain sides.

MOUNTAINS

These mountains are tilted blocks like those we saw in Oregon, but higher. Some of their rocks are hardened magmas and others are dark lava, or basalt. Most of them, however, are beds of limestone, sandstone, and shale that settled in ancient seas. They were tilted so much and pushed upward so far that they now form ranges that are 2,000 to 2,800 feet higher than the old lake bottom. Beds in the steepest ranges almost stand on end.

These blocks are not quite so young, for frost and water from sudden, hard rains have worn them into separate mountains. Other ranges have reached middle age. There's a big one near Great Salt Lake, for the Wasatch Mountains are a tilted block 130 miles long and 4,000 to 7,800 feet higher than desert flats across the lake. They also force the air upward, cooling it and turning its moisture into snow or rain. This water enables forests to grow; it also flows down canyons and is used to irrigate farms. It is said that each acre of farm land in Utah needs water that falls upon seven acres of block mountains. Dry farms in Montana, Wyoming, New Mexico, and other Western states also are irrigated with water that falls upon high ranges. Some are blocks and others are not, but all make moisture fall from the air as it blows across them.

But let's get back to changing block mountains in the Great Basin. The Wasatches are middle-aged because frost and streams have worn them into ridges and peaks divided by narrow canyons. We see other middle-aged blocks in Nevada. They are not so bare nor steep as the mountains west of Great Salt Lake; more bushes and trees grow upon them, and more creeks run down their sides. Those creeks have washed sand, gravel, and boulders into the valleys, spreading them out in wide slopes. Such slopes seem rough when we drive across them, but from a distance they look surprisingly smooth. They seem to cover the foot of each range, so that the mountains rise steeply from bare, gentle slopes.

From Nevada we go to the deserts of southern California and southwestern Arizona. Here we find wide, sloping valleys separated by ranges which are so old that they don't look like tilted blocks at all. Many are not even mountains, but have been worn down into rows of brown, cone-shaped hills. Some stand out like small islands among smooth, gravelly slopes.

Once these mountains were as steep and high as the ranges in northwestern Utah. But weathering made some rocks break, while others crumbled into sand grains. Then snow on the ranges melted, and hard rains like those we call cloudbursts fell almost every spring. Their water ran swiftly across the bare slopes, gathering into streams that rushed down every low place. They washed sand and broken stones away, using them to wear ravines where the rocks were soft or weak.

We may draw one diagram to show what the desert mountains looked like while they still were young. An-

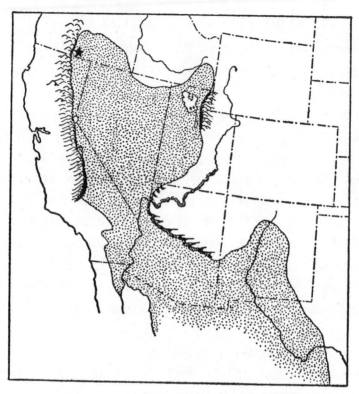

BLOCK MOUNTAINS HAVE CHANGED

The dotted part of this map shows where block mountains are found in North America. On the west is the Sierra Nevada, a block 400 miles long. The Wasatch Range forms part of the eastern border, near Great Salt Lake. A star marks the very young blocks near Upper Klamath Lake, in Oregon.

In the upper picture on the opposite page we see a slice through three block ranges. They are young, for their faulted sides are smooth and water is just beginning to wear ravines.

Slowly the ranges become middle-aged, as we see in the second drawing. The ravines have become canyons that divide the blocks into separate mountains. Broken rocks are piling up at the foot of every cliff.

At last the ranges grow old, turning into "island" peaks that are shown in the lower drawing. They are almost covered by slopes of broken rock, which also hide the broad benches left as the blocks were worn away.

other diagram shows what happened as rocks kept on breaking to pieces and as streams that flowed after storms carried more broken rocks away. They turned ravines into canyons, divided long cliffs into separate ridges, and wore sloping shelves or benches when they spread out at the foot of each mountain range. We notice, too, that those shelves were worn from the tilted blocks, making the mountains narrower. In some places the shelves are two or three times as wide as the worn ranges.

But what happened to the broken stones? At first they were washed all the way to the valleys. There the water left them as it sank into the ground, building slopes like those we saw in Nevada. In time the valley bottoms were covered, and floods began to spread their loads over the sloping shelves. They also piled rubbish up in fan-shaped heaps that ran far up the mouths of canyons.

Thus the block ranges became very old, as they are today. Their valleys are filled and the shelves are covered—but rocks go right on crumbling, and water continues to run downhill after every storm. It makes cliffs lower and cuts ridges to pieces; it makes the shelves just a bit wider by wearing the mountains away. It also spreads pebbles across wide slopes, piles them up in canyons, and fills low places between the peaks. Thus the oldest blocks turn into chains of peaks that look like pointed islands in a sea of pebbles and sand.

CHAPTER IX

Glaciers and the Ice Age

As YOU CLIMB or ride across high mountains you notice that the air becomes cool. Although it was warm and quiet in valleys, it is chilly on slopes above the trees. When you go still higher, you come to meadows or ridges where the air is cold and winds blow hard. Here the temperature is so low that snowbanks often last all summer. A little snow melts every day, of course, but winter comes before all is gone. Then clouds and storms bring more snow, which covers the ground and piles up on the partly melted banks.

Long ago, when these mountains first began, they were not much higher than hills. Air at their tops was as warm as air in the valleys between them. But year after year the mountains were pushed or built upward. At last their peaks and ridges became so high that snow could not completely melt, even in July and August.

A long time after this happened the climate began to

change. Summers became a week or two shorter; winters grew longer and colder. From October until April or May drifts of white snow covered the high places and filled every low basin or valley. The drifts piled so deeply that summer sunshine could melt only its topmost layers. This allowed the snow to settle and pack, much as a snowball packs when you warm it and press it with your hands. Then most of the melted snow froze again, forming ice crystals.

Year after year the drifts deepened and became larger, until they joined in snow fields that covered many acres. The snowflakes also kept on packing together, melting and freezing, forming layers of greenish-blue ice that began to spread across high places, or to creep downhill. We say that the snow fields turned into glaciers, which are ice "on the move."

There still are glaciers among mountains of the West, where snow piles up and becomes ice. Some have developed on high, rolling land, where they spread out for so many miles that we call them ice fields. Most ice fields move slowly, and they have surfaces that remind us of rolling plains. They are covered with coarse white snow that glistens in the sunshine.

Look at the edge of an ice field that lies near a road. In some places it slopes gently; in others it forms a steep bank that is made where blocks of ice break off and tumble over a cliff. But in one place a tongue of ice reaches out and travels down a valley. This valley

84

Granite in the Black Hills of South Dakota is crossed by cracks that allow weathering to divide the rock into slender pinnacles.

The Needle's Eye is a narrow hole worn through this pinnacle of granite.

Curved layers break off this weathered boulder in Colorado.

A muddy stream flows from this tongue-shaped glacier. Notice the piles of br
rocks and clay left as the ice melts.

Ice falls from the high cliffs, packs together, and forms a new glacier that n
down the valley toward Lake Louise, Alberta.

glacier is long and narrow, and it moves much more rapidly than the ice field from which it comes. We notice that it has split into long cracks called crevasses which divide the ice into huge blocks that look almost like waves. It is easy to see why such long, narrow glaciers are often called "rivers of ice."

Many valley glaciers do not come from ice fields, but begin on the sides of high mountains in caps of ice that cover peaks. You will see many ice streams of this kind on Mount Rainier, a huge, "dead" volcano in the state of Washington. There also are valley glaciers in Oregon, Alberta, Alaska, and other parts of the Northwest. Narrow ones often are almost covered with rocks which they have broken from mountains, or which fell from steep cliffs and landed upon the ice. On wide glaciers these rocks form long, dark ridges that wind along the moving ice.

Many glaciers of the Rocky Mountains lie in shallow, bowl-shaped valleys or cling to the sides of ridges and peaks. They seem to slide downhill rapidly, for there often is a wide crack between the packing, freezing snow and the moving ice. Most of these small glaciers are remains of much larger ones that have almost melted away. They are still melting, too, for water trickles down into their crevasses and runs away in creeks that splash from one ledge to another or drop in waterfalls.

Glaciers that cling to the sides of mountains often

come to the edges of cliffs, or to very steep slopes. When they do so, blocks of ice break away from their edges and slide or fall into valleys. If many large blocks fall, the broken ice may pack together and start to move again. In this way it forms a rebuilt, or "reconstructed," glacier. We look down upon one of these glaciers when we hike through the valley west of Lake Louise, Alberta. But we have to look closely to recognize it, for the ice is so thickly covered with stones that it looks like a stream of broken rock.

Ships that steam along the coast of Alaska sometimes go into Yakutat Bay. Here several huge valley glaciers come to the foot of the mountains and spread out near the shore, forming one sheet of ice known as Malaspina Glacier. It is sixty miles long, twenty-five miles wide, and moves very slowly. Sunshine has melted its topmost layers, and clay, sand, and stones now cover the surface. They even make rocky soil, where spruces and hemlocks grow on top of ice that is more than 100 feet thick.

Malaspina is as large and as flat as an ice field, but it formed in its own special way. We therefore call it a piedmont glacier, from an Italian word which means "at the foot of the mountains."

Piedmont glaciers once were found near Glacier National Park, at the foot of the Teton Mountains in Wyoming, and at other places in the West. They formed when ice came to the mouths of deep mountain canyons and spread out upon low, rolling land. Unfortunately for us, they melted a long time ago. All we can see of them is acres of low, rounded hills made of clay, gravel, and boulders that once covered the ice.

Still, we can tell what the old piedmont glaciers were like if we use our imaginations. Climb a hill near the Teton Mountains, look around, and put your imagination to work. Streams of ice come down those canyons and spread out when they reach the valley. The ice grinds, pushes, and cracks; its surface is covered with heaps and ridges of broken stone. As the ice melts, those ridges become thicker, until the glacier can hardly be seen. Except that it has no grass and trees, it looks almost exactly like the land around the hill on which we are standing. We have to remind ourselves that the glacier is only imaginary, since its ice became water and ran away thousands of years ago.

As we look at real glaciers among the mountains, we cannot see them move. But scientists have proved that they do and even have measured their speed. Small glaciers in the Rockies travel eight to fifteen inches per day, but big ones among mountains of Alaska move four to twelve feet. The speediest glacier of all is one that moves down the rocky coast of Greenland at a rate of fifty to seventy feet in a day. That is as far as "ice streams" of the Rockies go in a whole month!

People sometimes say that glaciers flow, as if they were made of water or syrup. But glaciers are formed of countless crystals of ice, which are almost as hard as the mineral crystals we found in granite and marble. You know that solid granite will not flow down a mountain side or valley.

A glacier really moves in three different ways, all at the same time. First of all, its ice slips and slides. Some layers of ice slip past others; layers at the bottom of the glacier slide down mountain sides and valleys. When a glacier melts, you can see where it slid over ridges and ledges.

While a glacier is sliding, its surface melts. Water runs over the ice and trickles down into cracks. At the bottom of these cracks the water freezes, which means that it swells as it hardens into ice. The ice presses against the sides of the cracks and helps push the glacier downhill.

Water and pressure help in another way. The surfaces of crystals melt, letting them roll or turn before they freeze again. When they turn, they move forward a tiny part of an inch. That may not seem important—but crystals can melt, move, and freeze millions of times while a glacier moves downhill.

Do these different ways of moving puzzle you? They also puzzle the scientists who study glaciers, for no one knows exactly how the movements work nor which one is most important. So don't bother about them too much nor try too hard to figure them out. Just remember that glaciers move because they slide, because their ice melts and freezes, and because crystals turn over and over millions upon millions of times.

As we look at glacier after glacier we notice that every one is smaller than it used to be. It is shorter and its ice is thinner. Some glaciers have melted away, leaving empty valleys and canyons, or piles of broken-up rock like the hills east of the Teton Mountains.

There was a time, however, when ice sheets covered whole ranges, when valley glaciers pushed their way to the plains, and when thick sheets of ice spread as far south as Kansas and New York. They filled canyons such as the Niagara Gorge and moved right over mountains as high as the Catskills in New York.

This cold part of the earth's history is known as the Ice Age. It began almost 2,000,000 years ago, when the climate grew cold and glaciers began to form. Those glaciers became larger and larger, till they filled almost every valley and covered all except the highest mountains. Other glaciers formed on lower lands, too. In time they covered North America from the Arctic Ocean to Kentucky, and from the Rocky Mountains to Newfoundland.

But cold weather and glaciers did not last through the whole Ice Age. In time the climate became warm— so warm that the ice melted. We say that an interglacial epoch set in. It was a part of the Ice Age that came between great glaciers.

MOUNTAINS

The epoch lasted thousands of years, while the weather became milder and milder. Trees grew upon the mountains again, while flowers bloomed on sunny slopes. Birds, insects, and beasts became common. Herds of wild horses roamed across the plains; hairy elephants called mammoths tramped through the deep valleys. Some of them even climbed the mountains, crossing passes on their way from one valley to another.

What happened after that? The interglacial epoch came to an end in another great cold spell. It killed plants and drove animals southward, while glaciers covered the country again. There were at least three epochs of warmth and four cold ones before the Ice Age finally came to an end.

But has it really ended? We feel sure that it has when we see glaciers melting into water that rushes down streams or tumbles over falls. It runs away much faster than ice can move forward, and faster than new ice can form from snow that has fallen in winter. It makes the glaciers smaller and shorter, until some of them are not much more than thick, partly frozen snowbanks.

Yes, glaciers are melting away and the Ice Age seems to have ended. But we can't be absolutely sure. We think about this as a cold storm howls across the mountains in August, when the weather is still hot at home. Here we shiver in woolen clothes and leather jackets, even though we have a camp fire. Ice covers pools every morning, and the mountain tops are white with snow.

A few flakes fall on the campground, along with sleet and some very chilly rain.

The Ice Age probably has ended. But if it were going to come back, isn't this just the way in which we'd expect it to begin?

CHAPTER X

The Scratched Boulder's Story

On ONE OF OUR TRIPS we hike through a valley—a deep one with very steep sides. Was it ever filled by a glacier—or can we tell? And what have glaciers done to ridges and peaks in the mountains near by?

While we puzzle over these questions, our trail passes low mounds that are made of gravel and boulders. Some of the rocks are oval and smooth, but others have jagged edges. We find one that is rounded on one side but is almost flat on the other. Dozens of deep, sharp scratches run across its surface.

This scratched boulder once was part of a peak which still stands at the head of the valley. When the Ice Age came, a glacier formed near the tip of this mountain. At first, of course, the glacier was small, but it became larger and longer every year. At last it reached to the foot of the peak and pushed its way down the valley, till it came to the bare, windy plains.

Boulders worn and rounded by the ice lie on this smooth glacial pavement in the Sierras near Cisco, California.

Peaks cut and steepened by ice in Glacier National Park, Montana. This is near the long lake shown in the colored frontispiece.

A piedmont glacier formed near the Teton Mountains in Wyoming, making these low hills of drift.
(*Union Pacific Railway.*)

At the right is a scratched boulder. Below we see a road cut in coarse glacial drift.

THE SCRATCHED BOULDER'S STORY

As the glacier moved, its ice caught hold of rocks on the surface and pushed them along with it. Ice also worked down into every crack, where it pried, pushed, and shoved till it loosened beds of stone. Block after block was pried and pulled out and was carried away by the ice.

The scratched boulder began as one of those blocks. At first it was as large as a motor truck and weighed hundreds of thousands of pounds. Yet the glacier loosened it and took it away without the least difficulty. The ice also carried smaller stones that fell from the mountain side. Some of them rolled or slipped into cracks that went deep down into the glacier. Others stayed near the surface till they were buried under layers of snow.

Winding this way and that, the glacier moved down the valley where the scratched boulder now lies. The ice moved faster at some places than at others; it broke into "falls" as it went down steep grades, and spread out when the valley widened. Layers slipped over other layers, and the whole thick mass squeezed together when it went around curves.

All these different movements pushed, pulled, and twisted the big stone. They also broke pieces from it, and from the other blocks of rock. Every one of those pieces was held firmly in the moving ice. It pushed them against each other, rubbing small pieces against big ones, and breaking them into chips. It ground the chips into sand and clay, which smoothed and rounded the larger rocks just as sandpaper smooths a piece of wood. Then the ice scraped rough rocks against the smooth ones, making deep scratches and grooves.

All these things happened to the block of stone as the glacier carried it down the valley. The glacier also broke more and more pieces from it, making it smaller and smaller. At last it became a boulder, with curved sides and rounded corners.

Then something new happened, for ice forced the boulder down against the rocky bottom of the valley. Though the boulder was hard, rocks under the glacier were harder. They scraped it flat on one side and ground its edges away; then their jagged parts cut into its face, making scratches several inches long. This happened over and over again, as ice turned the stone about and pushed it down the valley. If such treatment had lasted a few years longer, the scratched boulder would have been worn down into a small pebble.

But while the boulder was making its rough trip in the ice, things were happening in the world outside. First the climate began to change again—and this time it became warmer. Less snow fell and froze in the winter months, and summers became longer, with days that were really hot. Sunshine melted the glacier's ice faster than it could form from banks of snow.

You can guess what this did to the glacier. It kept on moving down the valley, but its ice melted away faster than it went forward. It melted most rapidly at the lower edge, which seemed to creep backward, making the glacier shorter. A river of muddy water flowed from the melting ice, rushing down the valley to the plains. This river carried mud, sand, and small boulders from the glacier, spreading them out in deposits which are called outwash.

But what about the boulder? It kept moving forward until it came to the edge of the glacier. There it lay when the ice melted and left it on the ground. The melting ice also dropped millions of other boulders, pebbles, sand grains, and tiny particles of clay. All were mixed together in a deposit of glacial drift.

In one place, however, the ice was so clean that it could not leave a drift deposit. Instead, we find the bare bedrock over which the old glacier moved. It is scraped as clean as a pavement and is covered with scratches made by rocks that were rubbed against it.

Scratched boulders, drift, and glacial pavement tell us that ice once filled this valley, though it melted and disappeared long ago. But other things tell us of ancient glaciers, too. Let us find out what they are.

We first look at valleys and the mountains around them. Before the Ice Age began, each valley had sloping sides, and its mouth was shaped like a huge letter V. The mountains also had sloping sides and broad, rounded ridges. They looked a good deal like the mature ranges of New York, which now are growing old.

MOUNTAINS

Glaciers of the Ice Age formed in those V-shaped valleys. There they pried and pulled out blocks of rock, making cliffs and deep basins. Miners often call those basins "half kettles," but geologists generally call them cirques. We can tell them by their steep, curved sides, which really are shaped very much like the sides of old-fashioned iron kettles.

As the glaciers grew larger they filled their cirques and moved on down the valleys. There they scraped, scratched, and dug out rocks. This deepened the valleys and made their sides steep. It also changed their V-shape to that of a broad U.

Big glaciers, of course, dug faster and deeper than small ones that came from side valleys. While ice covered the land this difference did not show. As the glaciers melted, however, little valleys were left "hanging" above the steep sides of big ones. When creeks flow to the edges of those cliffs, they tumble over in waterfalls or cascades. Yosemite Falls, in California, drop more than 2,500 feet from the mouth of a hanging valley.

While ice was changing the shapes of valleys, it made the mountains rugged and steep. We can see this where

---

HOW GLACIERS CHANGED A VALLEY

On the opposite page the first drawing shows a stream-worn valley with V-shaped sides, as it was when the Ice Age began. A huge glacier then filled the valley, while small ones came from near-by mountains. For thousands of years the ice pried, dug, and scraped. When it finally melted, the valley had become a deep canyon whose sides remind us of a wide U.

several glaciers cut cirques on both sides of a ridge. The ridge became narrower and steeper as the cirques became larger and deeper. At last only a jagged wall remained, with cliffs so steep that even mountain goats sometimes cannot climb them.

In other places, three or four glaciers cut cirques on different sides of one mountain. Farther and deeper they dug, until they left only a narrow peak shaped like a pyramid. The Swiss call such peaks "horns," but horn peaks also are found in North America. One of the most beautiful is Mount Assiniboine, which is two days' ride or hike from the town of Banff, Alberta.

Mount Assiniboine still has some of its glaciers, and so do other horn peaks in the United States. Many, however, are perfectly bare except when snow covers them in winter. Yet their shapes show that glaciers made them, just as drift and scratched boulders prove that glaciers once filled U-shaped valleys where we now find lakes and pine trees.

CHAPTER XI

Tree Pioneers and Settlers

WHEN GLACIERS of the Ice Age melted, many mountains and valleys were left bare. They also were cold and windy, with storms that blew clouds of dust across the barren slopes. Soon, however, plants began to grow, just as they had done during the interglacial epochs. They even ventured upon piles of drift near the melting glaciers.

Shrubs such as willows were the first of these plant pioneers. Then came flowers that could stand both wind and cold. Pines and other trees appeared, growing in green clumps. Those clumps became forests that spread farther and farther as the ice disappeared.

Today the glaciers are almost gone, except from northern peaks and ranges. Yet the mountains still have tree pioneers. Some live in places that are too rocky, too windy, or too cold for less hardy kinds. Others grow where old forests have been destroyed, making shelter

99

for other species that must have protection from sun and howling winds.

Shall we see how two kinds of pioneer trees get along where many others would die? Then let us visit a steep, stony ridge near the edge of the Northern Rockies. Here wind whistles across the slopes, even on bright summer days. It also does whirligigs in ravines and takes clouds of dust from bare places. On bad days it whips against weather-beaten trees that grow among coarse blocks of stone.

These trees, called limber pines, are the first of our pioneers. They came from seeds which the wind found in a valley and carried up to the ridge. Most of the seeds were blown over the ridge and away to the plains, but a few dropped in damp corners where they were able to sprout. They sent their roots down into the ground, while their stems grew up among the big stones. Thus the seedlings were sheltered from gales until they became several years old. By that time they could bend to and fro in the wind and were too strong to be killed by it.

Year after year the limber pines grew, becoming thick, sturdy trees with silvery gray bark. Their narrow leaves, or needles, were two or three inches long and grew in bundles of five. Cones four to ten inches long hung from the ends of their branches. The cones took almost two years to ripen and turn brown. They then

Mount Assiniboine, in the Canadian Rockies, is a famous horn peak. Notice that a glacier still clings to the mountain side.

Limber pine with short, thick trunk and umbrella-shaped branches.

A tall, straight Engelmann spruce.

Limber pine on a windy height grows close to the ground.

opened and dropped their seeds, which were blown away by the wind as it whistled along the ridge.

Would you like to see how these pioneer trees fit themselves to different conditions? Then suppose we hike along a trail that starts in a quiet, sheltered valley. Here the limber pines grow tall and straight, with trunks as much as eighty feet high. We have to look at their cones and count the needles in one bunch to tell them from some other trees.

Our trail soon climbs to the ridge and the pile of broken rocks. Here the pines have thick, short trunks and tops that spread out like umbrellas. Their branches cannot grow upward, for gales that blow twenty feet above the ground would whip their ends into shreds. One tree is twenty inches thick and only nineteen feet tall. It probably is three hundred years old, and it never will be much larger than it is today.

As we climb still higher the wind becomes so strong that we gasp when we walk against it. It has bent all the limber pines in one direction, twisting their branches about until they are almost streamlined. It has driven sand against their trunks, too, wearing their bark away. Many trees have lost so much bark that they died, though their gray trunks are still standing. The tough, twisted wood will not decay for many, many years.

At last we come to the top of the ridge, where the wind is a howling gale. Here the limber pines hardly grow upward at all. Instead, their trunks creep along the ground, while their branches twist over each other and around sharp stones. From a distance they look like clumps of bushes, not like trees that were growing long before the first white man explored the Rocky Mountains.

We call limber pines pioneers because they are the first trees to grow on windy slopes, and because they get along at timber line, which is as high as trees of any kind can live. In fact, that is where we must go to see them on many mountains in Colorado, Oregon, and California. In Montana, however, limber pines are common in windy valleys and on ridges near the edge of the plains. Life seems quite as hard down there as it is upon peaks and passes.

Lodgepole pines are pioneers in a different way. They are tall trees that grow in many places from seashore to timber line, and from Alaska to the Black Hills and Mexico. They have brownish-gray bark, two needles in a bunch, and cones an inch or two in length that are fastened close to their branches. Young trees are so slender and straight that Indians still use them as poles for their lodges, or tepees.

We find some pioneer lodgepoles on bare peaks, where they grow in cracks. Other young pioneers are more important, for they live in a desolate valley where a forest fire killed all other trees many years ago. It destroyed the lodgepole pines, too, but it could not harm the short, hard cones that clung to their branches. In-

Lodgepole
Pine

Limber Pine

Western Larch

Western
Hemlock

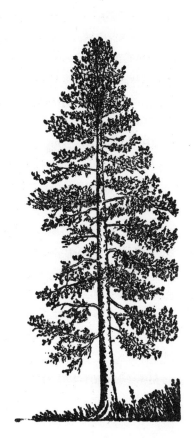

stead, heat from the fire made those cones begin to open. Soon their seeds fluttered down to the scorched ground, where they grew into these young trees. In time the lodgepoles will make a shady forest in which spruces and firs can find shelter when they come back to the valley.

One tree that comes to lodgepole woods is the western yellow, or ponderosa, pine. Since it follows the hardy pioneers, we may call it a settler. It grows tall, with a thick, straight trunk that is covered with red-brown or salmon-colored bark, crisscrossed by blackish cracks. Three yellowish-green needles grow in each bunch and are five to ten inches long. Cones form at the ends of branches and hang down; they are green or purple when they are young, but turn brown as their seeds ripen.

Ponderosa pines grow from British Columbia to the Black Hills and Mexico, especially in rather dry valleys. In southern Oregon and California you also will see their relatives, which are known as Jeffrey pines. These trees have larger cones and darker bark that divides into smaller pieces. But if you can't be sure of these differences, smell a deep crack in the bark. The Jeffrey pine has an odor of pineapple, but the ponderosa pine does not.

If you have camped or hiked in the North Woods you have seen tall, straight white pines. Their Western relatives are straight and tall, too, with blackish bark that breaks into small sections. Their blue-green needles are two to four inches long and grow in bundles of five. Slender cones, six to ten inches in length, hang in clusters from the ends of branches. Small limbs are whitish gray, but the tree gets its name from its white wood, which makes very fine lumber. Western white pines grow among mountains from Canada to southern California and as far eastward as Montana. You can tell them easily by their long needles and very dark bark.

Pines are evergreens, for their needle-shaped leaves stay on the branches all year. Many persons call all evergreens pines, yet several other kinds are found along every mountain highway or trail. Those pointed trees, for example, are spruces; notice how their cones hang downward, while their branches grow out like the spokes of a wheel. Their needles are stiff and pointed, pricking sharply when you close your hand around them.

One kind of spruce grows all the way from the Yukon to Arizona, and from the Black Hills of South Dakota almost to the Pacific coast. In spite of this, it is not a pioneer, for it settles in forests of lodgepole pines. It becomes common as the pines die out, much as farmers and townspeople settled in the West after the frontiersmen grew old or moved on to other regions.

Firs may be even thinner and more pointed than spruces, but their flat leaves do not prickle and their cones stand upright. Their bark is covered with balsam blisters, which are filled with clear, sticky resin.

MOUNTAINS

Alpine firs often grow in valleys, where they become slender trees that remind us of church steeples. We recognize them by their ash-gray bark and their upright purple cones, which ooze big drops of resin that glisten in the sunshine. On high slopes the trees become stunted, and they finally spread along the ground almost like limber pines.

White firs are not so slender and pointed, and they do not grow on high mountains. They do best in valleys and on north slopes of mountains, where they may grow 150 feet high. Their bark is ash gray and hard; on old trees it is four to six inches thick and breaks into rough ridges. Young needles are yellowish green, but old ones become bluish. The cones generally are pale green, and are much thicker than those of the alpine fir.

Douglas firs are not firs at all, but have characters that belong to a whole series of trees. They are distinguished by the three-pointed "whiskers" on their cones, which are not very large. Young trees have smooth gray bark, but on old ones it becomes reddish brown and as much as ten inches thick. It protects the trees so well that they can live through forest fires which destroy pines, spruces, and real firs.

Hemlocks are evergreens with soft, rather flat needles and small cones. Four kinds, or species, live in North America: two in the North Woods and mountains of the East and two among valleys and ranges of the West. The mountain hemlock lives on high ridges and slopes;

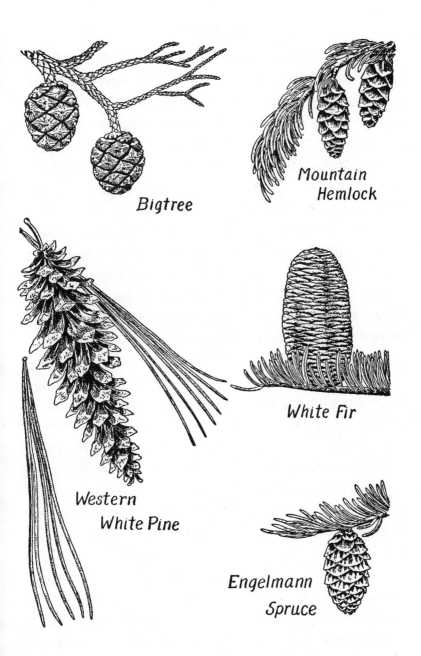

Bigtree

Mountain
Hemlock

Western
White Pine

White Fir

Engelmann
Spruce

you can tell it by its needles, which grow in star-shaped clusters, and by its little cones. The western hemlock is a much larger tree whose needles spread out sidewise. It grows on mountains near the Pacific coast and in valleys among the Rockies of Montana. Many trees become 200 feet high, with trunks five or six feet in thickness. These huge hemlocks are four hundred and fifty to five hundred years old.

The real giants among evergreens are the bigtrees, which live in the Sierra Nevada of California. They are tall, thick trees with reddish-brown bark, leaves that look like tiny scales, and small, solid cones. Many are 250 to 280 feet high and twelve to seventeen feet thick, while a few are much larger.

Bigtrees are related to the sequoias that lived in Colorado and Wyoming millions of years ago. But they are not pioneers. Instead, they just manage to live in special basins or valleys where conditions are exactly right. Even there they grow in scattered groves, not in thick forests as other trees often grow.

If we stay in the mountains until autumn we find that some "evergreens" actually shed their needles and become as bare as elms or maples. These are the larches, or tamaracks, which grow in valleys where forest fires have killed even the lodgepole pines. Larches can be recognized by their fluffy, pale green needles which grow in brushy clusters that are fastened to brown stubs. There may be thirty or forty needles in a single brush.

Cones of the Jeffrey pine.

Cones, needles, and trunks of the ponderosa, or western yellow, pine.

The tips of a young Engelmann spruce.

Upright, sticky cones of the alpine

Larch trees beside a lake in Canadian Rockies.

Mountain hemlocks on Lassen Peak.

Young Douglas fir cones.

TREE PIONEERS AND SETTLERS

The western larch is the one you are likely to see in valleys among the mountains. It has a straight, tall trunk and reddish-brown bark that is thick and dark near the ground. Its branches are short and thin, and its needles are yellowish. The alpine larch, however, is a small tree with many branches and rather dark bark that grows near timber line. You will know it by its shape and its bluish-green needles.

While we are looking for evergreens, we also find other trees. Quaking aspens, or poplars, live on many slopes, even where the wind is so strong that their trunks twist along near the ground. They have greenish-silvery bark with a bitter taste, but hungry elk often eat it. Their name comes from their flat, broad leaves which tremble, or quake, in every breeze.

Tall trees beside creeks are black cottonwoods. Their leaves are longer and more pointed than those of aspens, and their thick bark cracks into coarse ridges. Black cottonwoods that live among mountains near the Pacific coast grow more than 100 feet high, with trunks three or four feet thick. Other kinds, or species, that grow in valleys of the southwestern mountains also become very large.

Where trees grow we also find bushes. Alders form thickets beside streams where mountain visitors like to fish. Dwarf maples live on dry, sunny slopes. Their leaves, which have many different shapes, turn bright red in the autumn.

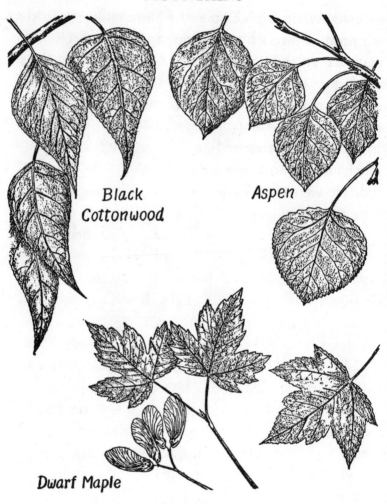

Black
Cottonwood

Aspen

Dwarf Maple

Both alders and maples are settlers, for they live
among trees which give them shelter and just enough
shade. For a pioneer we choose the white dryad, whose
leaves have rounded teeth and are woolly on the underside. The dryad really is a woody shrub, but it grows

on cold Arctic-Alpine heights where bushes would be whipped to pieces by the wind. So the plant grows in mats six or eight inches high, nestling among sharp stones that have been broken by frost. There it blooms and gets along very well, though we shiver and put on sweaters when we stop to take its picture.

We must rank as settlers, too, for we seem to need much more warmth and shelter than the mountains provide for their plant pioneers!

CHAPTER XII

Plants from Valleys to Peaks

PEOPLE WHO TALK about the mountains sometimes call them "harsh" or "severe." But they don't seem harsh to us as we drive through a valley on our way to a national park. Up and around we go, winding through green woods till our road stops at the foot of a peak. Here we camp among tents and trailers in a grove of tall pines. Surely nothing could be more pleasant than this campground at the foot of snowcapped peaks!

We say so to a ranger in a forest-green uniform. "Yes," he agrees, "this *is* pretty nice. But the mountains aren't all like this campground, and things that live easily here wouldn't get along very well on those high cliffs. If you like, I'll tell why at the camp-fire program tonight. We'll start out with some songs, and then I'll talk about life zones.

"You don't know what life zones are? Then be sure

*Beargrass blooms beside a highway that winds past a horn peak
in Glacier National Park.*

to come over and find out. They'll show you why I say that the mountains aren't so pleasant everywhere as they are right here. They also will explain lots of things you'll see as you hike along the trails."

We find out that life zones really are a good deal like building zones in a city. Building zones are arranged according to rules which say there shall be stores in one place, factories in another, and houses in a third part of town. Life zones, however, have no printed rules. They depend on sunshine, snow, cold weather, winds, and other things that decide where plants and animals may live. Creatures that fit each set of conditions are found together, just as houses that fit one special rule are put into one building zone.

We may not think about life zones when we are at home, for most of us live in places where zones are so wide that we seldom go from one to another. In the Mississippi Valley, for example, we should have to travel from New Orleans to Illinois to cross a single life zone. But a day's trip in the mountains may take us through three or four zones and back again. These are as many as we could see on a trip from Pittsburgh to Labrador, or along the Pacific coast from San Francisco to northern Alaska.

Let's look at several different life zones, paying special attention to their plants. We approached the mountains over foothills where buffalo herds used to roam. Then we came to a broad valley, where we noticed aspens with silvery green bark, strong-smelling sage-brush, and wild rose bushes. Indians were camped near a creek, picking dark blue serviceberries which look like those that grow on shadbushes away back in New England. We are not surprised when the ranger says that the hills and valley belong to a strip of country known as the Transition Zone. "It's about halfway between the North and the South, the East and the West, the open plains and the mountains. It makes us think of a newly built suburb, where city houses are mixed with fields and a few farm buildings."

"City" plants from the mountains are easy to pick out; they include lodgepole pines, Douglas firs, and a few limber pines that grow on specially windy foot-hills. "Farm" plants from the plains show plainly, too. We notice black-eyed Susans, white yarrows with their feathery leaves, and purple-flowered rough asters that bloom in late summer. Sagebrush grows on many dry slopes. The commonest kind has gnarled stems and small, silvery leaves that end in three blunt teeth. It is found on dry plains and in mountain valleys south of central Montana and eastward to Colorado and the Black Hills. Near Northern mountains we find sages whose leaves are pointed, though they also are silvery gray. Indians often use these plants to make medicine.

Our camp is in the Canadian Zone, which resembles the North Woods of Canada, though its trees are not quite the same. In Colorado the zone has forests of pon-

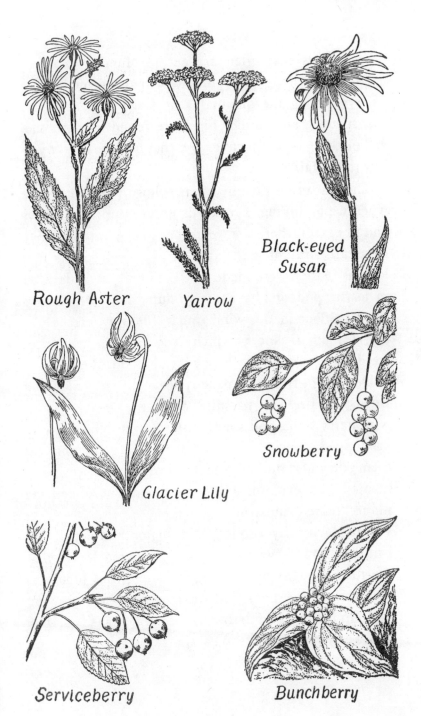

Rough Aster

Yarrow

Black-eyed
Susan

Glacier Lily

Snowberry

Serviceberry

Bunchberry

derosa pines that often are cut for lumber. Farther north we find lodgepole pines, which also grow in high valleys among the mountains of California. Douglas firs, spruces, and limber pines are found in this zone, and quaking aspens form groves that become bright yellow in the fall.

The Canadian Zone has many flowers which we see when we go hiking. Fireweeds grow in open meadows and in places where the woods have been burned. They have tall, straight stalks and purplish-red flowers that look as if they were made of silk. Their seeds develop in narrow pods and have tufts of fluffy down which help them to float in the wind. Such "flyaway" seeds can travel long distances, which may explain why fireweeds are found in the East as well as the West.

Dew drops from cow parsnip leaves as we walk along woodsy trails. The parsnips are large, coarse plants with hairy stalks and small white flowers that grow in flat-topped bunches. Indians roast the roots and eat them; they also put stalks on their altars in sacred ceremonies. This explains why some mountaineers call the plants "sacred rhubarb."

The glacier lily also is called dogtooth violet. It has bright yellow flowers and smooth, pointed leaves that are four to eight inches long. Glacier lilies bloom as soon as the snow melts, and you may find them growing through the edges of drifts that remain on shady slopes. Bears dig up the plants to eat their bulbs.

Dwarf willows, less than six inches high.

Alder leaves and "cones."

White dryads on an Arctic-Alpine slope.

The common three-toothed sage.

Flowers and buds of a fireweed.

Indian paintbrush beside a log.

PLANTS FROM VALLEYS TO PEAKS

Indian paintbrush has flowers that really are mostly leaves. The plants grow in bunches, with straight stalks; their flowers are yellow, orange, pink, or various shades of red. The prettiest ones are orange or scarlet and grow on rather dry slopes.

When beargrass is not in bloom, it looks like bunches of long, wiry grass that grows on sunny slopes and in valleys. Every few years these plants send up tall stalks with bunches of cream-colored flowers at the top. When you look at these flowers closely, you will find that they really are small lilies with bright yellow pollen that comes off when you shake them.

So here are three things to remember about beargrass: First, it is a special kind of lily, not a grass. Second, it does not bloom every year, which means that you will be very lucky to find a big patch in bloom. Third, bears don't eat beargrass stems nor their tough, wrinkled roots. Squaw grass actually is a better name for these plants. The women, or squaws, of some Indian tribes used to make strong baskets out of dried beargrass leaves.

Mariposa, in Spanish, means butterfly, and mariposa lilies on a slope do look like butterflies bobbing above the grass. Each plant has one narrow leaf and a blossom at the top of a long stalk. Some kinds are cream-colored with purple spots at the center, but others are yellow or pale purple. Some people call them tulips, while a kind that grows on dry slopes in Utah is known as the sego lily. Pioneers often ate its bulbs when they ran out of other food.

Wild geraniums have leaves which are divided into narrow parts, or lobes. One species with small pink flowers lives in woods and thickets. Like a few other plants, it is found from the Pacific coast to the Atlantic and among hills as well as mountains. It has several common names, one of which is crane's-bill.

We see these flowers of the Canadian Zone as we hike or ride near camp. But one morning we take a trail that leads through a valley, climbs to a glacier, and goes on to a snowy peak. At first we cross a sunny meadow on which are several plants that grow in two or more zones. We notice serviceberries like those at the edge of the plains, and waxy white snowberries. False hellebore grows in patches. Its large, coarse leaves are pale, yellowish green; many of them have been eaten by insects. The small flowers are yellow or green.

Thimbleberries grow in damp, shady woods just beyond the meadow. The shrubs have white flowers and very large leaves that overlap almost like shingles. The fruit is bright red and looks somewhat like a raspberry. In fact, this plant is closely related to both blackberries and raspberries.

Bunchberries grow close to the ground in damp, shady places. They get their name from the fact that their bright scarlet berries grow in thick bunches. The

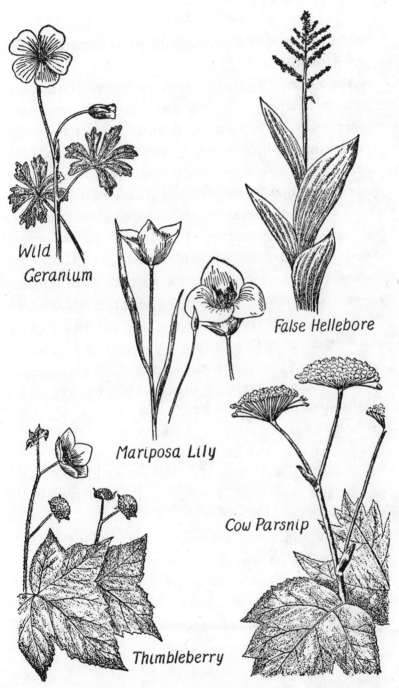

Wild Geranium

False Hellebore

Mariposa Lily

Cow Parsnip

Thimbleberry

leaves show that these pretty little shrubs are related to dogwoods of the East.

Soon our trail begins to climb, going up the mountain side in zigzags known as switchbacks. Higher and higher we go, while the trees become small and weather-beaten. Another hour of hiking brings us to the glacier, which looked sparkling white from the campground. Now we see that it really is a strip of dirty blue-green ice half covered with stones that have fallen from steep cliffs around it. A creek that flows from the ice turns into falls that tumble down the mountain.

Near the glacier are rocky slopes which look so much like the land near Hudson Bay that we call them the Hudsonian Zone. Here we find dwarf willows that are real bushes, even though they are less than a foot in height. Alpine firs grow close to the ground, where their twisted trunks wind among the rocks like the trunks of windbeaten limber pines. Red and white heather form green, springy mats. The red heather has bell-shaped blossoms, but those of the white heather look like tiny vases turned upside down. Yellow arnica blooms on a pile of glacial drift. Butterflies with peacock spots on their wings flutter about the flowers.

The butterflies stay where they are, but we go on. Soon our trail comes to a huge pile of broken rock where little pikas, or conies, skip about and call *Eek! Ee-eek!* in thin, squeaky voices. They look a bit like baby rabbits with round ears, short legs, and no tail.

Their grayish-brown fur makes them look like rocks when they sit still.

The pikas soon go back to work, cutting grass and other plants. One of them brings some arnica leaves to a flat rock and spreads them out in the sun. When his "hay" is dry he will store it under rocks, to be eaten in wintertime. For pikas run about and are hungry even when their houses are covered by six or eight feet of snow.

At last we come to the Arctic-Alpine Zone, where snowdrifts lie on the ground all year, as they do in northern Alaska and Greenland. A chilly wind blows from these drifts, though the sun is shining brightly. We shiver until we put on windbreaks or sweaters and find a sheltered place to lunch.

Lunch gives us a chance to rest. It is welcome, for climbing this mountain is much harder than walking in the valley near camp. Our breath became short an hour ago, while we were in the Hudsonian Zone. Our hearts beat harder, too, and we had to walk more slowly. One fellow-hiker complained of a headache; another had a nosebleed. We, ourselves, feel dizzy and gasp when we jump up suddenly. Life does not seem too easy here near the mountain top!

Life isn't easy, yet some things get along very well. We find patches of pioneer dryads and several kinds of "rock-breakers" that never grow in lower places. A little willow creeps along the ground, with branches that are three or four inches high. Carpet pinks, with bright flowers and tiny green leaves, grow in clumps where melting snowbanks moisten the ground. Little orange-and-gray plants called lichens cover a stone that stands up above a snowdrift.

The lichens are so dry and thin that they hardly seem to be alive. But there's no doubt about brown birds that hop on the snow, or the white mountain goat that is climbing from one ledge to another. He has been down to the Hudsonian Zone for breakfast, but the sunshine there has become much too warm for his shaggy coat. Soon he picks out a shady rock on the north side of a cliff and lies down. There he will keep cool and comfortable until near sunset, when he'll be ready for another meal of plants that grow near Arctic-Alpine snows.

CHAPTER XIII

Beasts and Fish of the Mountains

AFTER OUR TRIP to the Arctic-Alpine Zone we come back to camp on the lake shore. We feel tired, but are much too hungry to rest. Soon we have a fire crackling in the grate and are putting food from our grub box upon a long table.

That food looks mighty good to us, and to other things that live in the campground. While our bacon is broiling a ground squirrel comes up, sitting on his short hind legs to beg for raisins. Then two Rocky Mountain jays fly past and come back to teeter and chuckle on a branch just above our table. We admire their fluffy gray feathers and the way they seem to bounce through the air. But we aren't so well pleased when they swoop down to steal a piece of meat and a cookie. It's easy to see why these clownish birds are often called "camp robbers."

We forget the jays when a neighbor calls "Look!"

Two mule deer have walked into camp; we know them by their long ears, short tails, and their antlers whose prongs divide into Y's. Since it is summer, those antlers still are covered with velvety skin which makes them look much larger than they really are. They seem top-heavy when the deer bound away with queer, stiff-legged jumps.

If we were in mountains near the Pacific coast we should see Columbia blacktail instead of mule deer. Blacktails are small, neat-looking animals whose coats are reddish brown in summer, but are brown peppered with gray in winter. The tail is white on the underside and black or dark gray on the upper. In many places these deer become so tame that they come to camp-grounds every day, begging for candy and food.

We see two large kinds of deer when we take our next hike. One of these is the elk, which scientists like to call by its Indian name of wapiti. Male, or bull, elk are eight feet long, five feet high at the shoulder, and weigh 600 to 700 pounds. They have brown bodies with straw-colored rumps and very large antlers. The young ones, or calves, are covered with white spots which make them hard to see when they hide among bushes.

Long ago elk used to live on the plains and even among woods in the East. But hunters killed them and farmers drove them away, and now the elk spend their summers in the mountains or on high plateaus. People who drive along the Trail Ridge Road, west of Estes

Butterflies come to flowers that bloom in late summer.

Beargrass flowers show that they really are lilies.

Blue-green, yellow, and orange lichens are common on rocks.

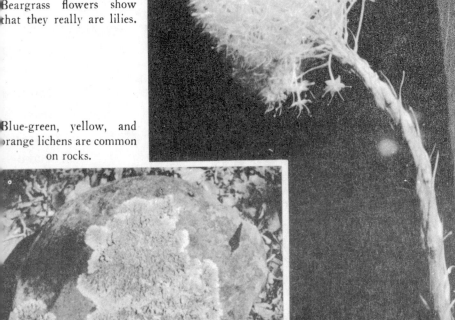

This bighorn lamb was bo[rn]
in a paddock, where he pla[yed]
on stumps instead of roc[ks.]

Bighorn sheep in Glac[ier]
National Park, Monta[na,]
after an early autumn sno[w.]
(Photo by Hilema[n)]

BEASTS AND FISH OF THE MOUNTAINS

Park in Colorado, sometimes see bands of elk on Hudsonian slopes that are far above timber line.

Moose, which like valleys with thick forests, are the largest deer in the world. A bull moose comes every morning to a lake not far from camp. He has a thick body with dark, shaggy hair, a long nose, and antlers that are wide and thick. A "bell" of skin on his throat bobs to and fro every time he moves his head. He nips twigs from willows and dwarf maples; then he wades into the lake and begins to eat water plants. We take his picture and go on, for a full-grown moose may become angry when people bother him. One fellow in camp forgot that rule. He spent two very uncomfortable minutes before the moose decided not to charge, but to hide in the woods.

On a rocky slope above our trail lives a band of ten or twelve bighorns, which are large, brown mountain sheep with stiff hair instead of wool. The females have short, thin horns; those of the males are thick and curved and are covered with wrinkly ridges. At this season the mothers and lambs stay together, but the males generally go off by themselves in herds of four or five.

When bighorn sheep are frightened they gallop along talus slopes, or jump from one ledge of rock to another so fast that they seem to bounce. Pads on their hooves keep them from slipping when they land upon smooth stones.

In national parks, where they are not hunted, big-horns become tame. They come to cabins for salt, eat hay which rangers get for their horses, and walk along the roads. The first time we went to Banff National Park our train stopped with a jerk just as it got into the mountains. Three bighorn rams were standing on the track—and there they stayed while the engineer tooted his whistle and the fireman waved a shovel at them. At last they stepped daintily upon a slope to the highway, where they stood while our train puffed and chugged away.

Bighorns often come to valleys of the Canadian Zone in winter, especially if park rangers give them food. But mountain goats like to spend the cold months on high ridges, where winds blow the snow away. This gives the goats a chance to find food, while their thick coats of white hair keep them warm. During bad storms they hide under ledges, or among big rocks.

As we watch a family of goats we notice that they walk slowly and almost never run. They step carefully from rock to rock; sometimes they stand on their hind legs and climb up steep ledges. Mothers teach their little ones, or kids, to climb or jump by pushing them. After a few lessons a tiny kid will go up or down the steepest cliff right behind its mother.

Walking across a high meadow, we come to a place where chunks of dirt have been dug out of the ground. This means that a bear has been digging ground squirrels, and we think the bear was a grizzly. We are sure when we find a big, wide track with marks made by straight claws. The grizzly itself is a huge, grayish-brown animal with thick fur and a wide face. It stands four feet high at the shoulder, weighs 700 to 800 pounds, and is strong enough to kill a moose without half trying. Yet it likes to eat fish, ground squirrels, and ants, as well as berries of several kinds.

Mother grizzlies generally have two cubs, which are happy, fluffy-looking fellows. They often hide in bushes or climb trees when their mother goes for food. If they come down before they are told, she gives them a few spanks with one of her big paws.

Many people who visit the mountains like to watch black bears that take food from garbage cans or beg beside the road. But such bears really are badly spoiled, and they often are dangerous, too. They bang and batter the garbage cans; they tear tents to pieces to get bacon; they break into trailers and cars. They have scratched and bitten many people, and their manners are much worse than those of an alley rat.

Really wild black bears are much more likable. They also eat berries, roots, ground squirrels, and mice, or catch trout in creeks. They mind their own business and bother no one; they are fun to meet. When we encounter black bears they often climb trees, but sometimes they gasp *Woof!* in surprise and run away as fast as they can. "Once I almost stepped on a bear," a ranger tells

Elk

Moose

Black Bear

Grizzly

128

us. "He was sitting in the trail with his mouth open, watching yellow butterflies. When he saw me he rolled over sidewise, landed on his feet with a bounce, and galloped into the woods. I had to ask a hiker for that special bruin's picture. How did we know it was the same bear? Because he came back to that same place the next day and watched the butterflies!"

Black bears are much smaller than grizzlies and have narrower faces. Their claws are curved instead of straight, which explains why they climb trees almost as well as squirrels do. Many black bears really are brown, and some are almost cream colored. But, except for their color, they are just like their dark relatives.

Small animals which are as greedy as bears often come into camp. One of these is the mantled ground squirrel, which some people call a chipmunk. It has one white stripe and two black ones on each side of its back and a whitish ring around each eye. It also is much larger than any chipmunk and does not fidget so much. It likes to fill its cheek pouches with nuts, crumbs, and other things. Then it runs away to store them in its burrow, but soon comes back for more.

These ground squirrels generally are born in May or early June, and by August they are big enough to take care of themselves. They eat so much that they become very fat, and begin their winter sleep in September. Those that live in cold mountains may not wake up until April comes.

At night we sometimes see a fluffy gray animal with a long tail, black eyes, and big round ears. "That's a pack rat," says an old-timer in the mountains. "He has a nest under those big rocks behind your tent. He has piled up bushels of sticks, weeds, chips, and other things, using them to build hallways and rooms. Perhaps he has some tin cans, too, and a few knives or spoons."

"Where did he get those?" we ask.

"From campers. That's how he gets his name—because he carries, or 'packs,' things away. Often he drops one thing and picks up another. Some people say he trades sticks or stones for tin cans, forks, or even cakes of soap. So they call him a trade rat."

Northern pack rats have bushy tails, and they run and jump about like squirrels. But their relatives that live among southwestern mountains look and act much more like real rats. They eat the green, pulpy joints of cactus plants and build their nests on the ground. If you find a big pile of rubbish under a cactus or spiny tree, you may be sure it is the home of a Southern pack rat.

Many trees among the mountains have bare yellow patches where their bark has been gnawed off. This was done by the yellow-haired porcupine, which is specially common in the Rockies of Colorado. You can tell him from the Eastern porcupine by the long, greenish-yellow hair that covers his sharp quills. He is peaceful, minds his own business, and never shoots his quills. If

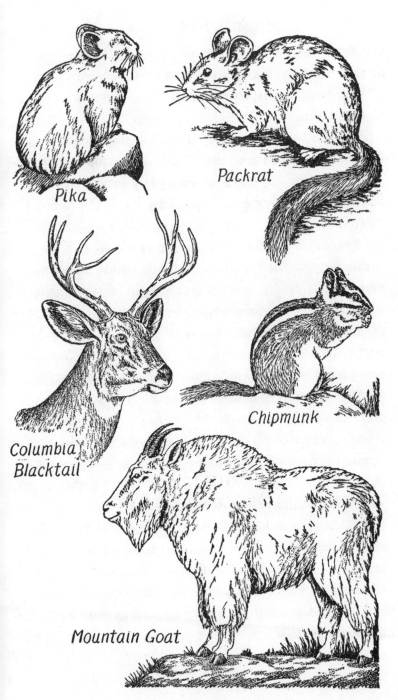

Pika

Packrat

Columbia
Blacktail

Chipmunk

Mountain Goat

you meet one of these animals he will climb a tree or crouch down on the ground with his nose between his paws. There he will stay as long as you are near enough to alarm him.

Porcupines gnaw on bark in the winter, when other food is scarce. In the summer they eat almost anything. They are specially fond of water-lily leaves, and they also like salt. They even will chew hard, dry wood if there is salt in it.

As we climb rocky slopes in the Hudsonian Zone we hear a long, shrill whistle. It is made by the hoary marmot, which really is a distant cousin of the Eastern woodchuck, or groundhog. The marmot is a shaggy animal about two feet long, with gray hair on the fore part of its body and brown hair behind. It lives in holes, eats plants of many kinds, and keeps a close watch for enemies. That long whistle is a signal that means "Someone's coming!" If you come too near, the animal will whistle very sharply and run to the nearest hole.

Hoary marmots are found from northern Montana to the Arctic, and as far east as Hudson Bay. Farther south you will see the yellow-bellied marmot, which also is called the rockchuck. It looks a good deal like the woodchuck, but has brighter colors. Instead of whistling it generally chirps loudly. You may think it is a bird until you see its furry body on a boulder near the trail.

Marmots, porcupines, pack rats, and ground squirrels do not look alike, yet they resemble each other in one

e yellow-haired porcupine
ound among mountains from
Black Hills to California.

ptarmigan beside a moun-
tain lake.

o mule deer with antlers
in velvet.

The Columbia ground squirrel
begs food and picks up crumbs
dropped by picnickers.

This hoary marmot, or
whistler, makes his home near
a barren pass.

The golden-mantled ground
squirrel is larger than any
chipmunk.

very important way. All nip off their food with four long, curved teeth at the front of their mouths. These teeth grow all the time, and are arranged so that their edges keep as straight and sharp as chisels. Indeed, one man who writes about animals has said that these creatures have chisel-teeth and belong to the "chisel-tooth tribe."

This tribe is a very big one. It includes mice, real rats, squirrels, and rabbits, as well as the pikas which we saw on our trip to the mountain top. The beaver is a member of the chisel-toothed tribe that has brown fur, a flat tail, and webbed feet. He can swim much faster than he walks, and spends most of his life in the water. Many beavers live in mountain valleys, where they build dams across creeks and eat the bark of aspens, cottonwoods, willows, and a few other trees. They make their houses of sticks mixed with dirt and grass and cover them with a layer of mud. Summer rains often wash this mud away, so that the houses look like piles of dead wood sitting in the water.

Many people go fishing on beaver dams, but others prefer a lake or a swiftly flowing creek. Here they may catch rainbow trout, which have many different colors. The prettiest ones are silvery gray with a red stripe on each side. They also have many small black spots, but their cheeks and bellies are rosy red and their throats are pink.

Rainbow trout once lived mostly in California, but

men have "planted" them in the lakes and streams of many other regions. They eat insects that live under water and others that fall into it. A rainbow trout has to eat and grow for six or eight years before it is large enough to catch, and big ones may be a dozen years old.

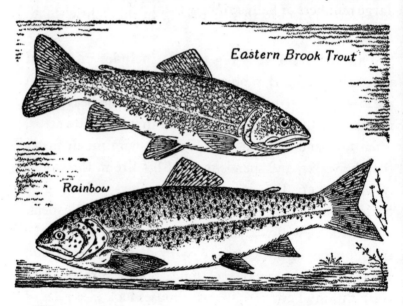

Eastern Brook Trout

Rainbow

When we hike to lakes in the rocky Hudsonian Zone, we often catch cutthroat trout or see them swimming in the clear water. They are silvery, olive, or steely gray with black spots, and get their name from their bright red lower jaws. Their flesh is red, too, and tastes a good deal like salmon. Cutthroats are natives of the Northern Rockies and live best in lakes whose water comes right from melting snowbanks.

Eastern brook trout also like high, cold lakes. They

are gray or olive, with red or gray spots which often have white borders. They lay their eggs in the fall, though other trout lay theirs in the spring. When brook trout go into creeks they stay in small, deep pools where they catch insects and little fish. Sometimes they eat large numbers of baby rainbow trout.

CHAPTER XIV

Birds in Four Life Zones

Many BIRDS, as well as beasts, live among the mountains. Let's look at them as we looked at plants—by going from one life zone to another till we come to an Arctic-Alpine peak.

We begin in the wide, sunny valley that is almost like the plains. Here robins and meadowlarks sing, while mourning doves fly up in front of our car and crows caw as they teeter on treetops. Soon a magpie calls *Squak, squa-ak!* as it perches upon a willow. It is a big black-and-white bird with rather short wings and a very long, black tail that tapers to a point. Magpies often eat mice, but most of their food is grasshoppers and other insects. They also are glad to get garbage, or to feed on animals that have been killed by automobiles.

Back at camp, in the Canadian Zone, Rocky Mountain jays come to our table two or three times every day. We can tell them from "camp robbers" of the North

Magpies

Woods by their white-topped heads, while a variety
found in states along the Pacific coast has white only on
the forehead. But they have the same habits as other
camp robbers, and even try to steal pancakes that weigh
almost as much as they do.

Chack-ah, chack-ah, chack! calls a jay with a blackish
body, blue back, and purplish wings and tail. People
who live in the mountains call him a bluejay, but he
really has been named for Georg Steller, a Russian
naturalist who went to Alaska many years ago. There
are several different varieties of Steller jays, each with
its own special colors. The one we see in the Northern

Rockies has a black head and a white spot above each eye and is called the black-headed jay. It is larger than the real Steller's jay, which lives near the Pacific coast.

These birds have crests of feathers on their heads. They like to fly to and fro in thick woods, squawking and screaming noisily. Sometimes they chase other birds, but they don't often quarrel with each other. They will eat almost anything, but most of them are too shy to steal food as the camp robbers do.

"I've just seen two fool-hens!" one hiker tells us. "They let me come right up close and didn't know enough to run away!"

The "fool-hens" are dusky grouse. This name comes from their bluish-gray feathers, which are almost black on the tail. They are tame because they live in a national park, where no one is allowed to kill them. Where dogs chase these grouse and hunters shoot them, they soon become very wild. So "fool-hens" are not foolish after all. Instead, they act just as they need to when they live in safe places and in others that are dangerous.

No one ever calls ouzels foolish, but many people do think they are queer. They are gray birds with short tails and rather long legs; we see them along creeks and rocky lake shores. Ouzels bob up and down almost like wrens, which explains why they often are called "dippers." When they are hungry they hunt young insects that live in the water. The birds dodge among stones, go

Ouzel

Pipit

into cracks, and drop down into pools, where they run along on the bottom. Then they bob up again with their beaks full of food and swiftly fly away.

Ouzels build round nests of moss among rocks near waterfalls, where spray keeps the moss moist and green. After the young birds leave the nest, they hop from one ledge to another until they are ready to fly. Most ouzels stay in their mountain homes all year, singing happily on days when the temperature is thirty or forty degrees below zero. They even dive and swim in streams that are almost covered with ice.

At night we hear horned owls talking to each other. *Hoo-hoo!* one will say in a hollow voice. *Hoo-hoo, hoo-*

ooh, hoo-hoo! another owl answers—or it may give a squeaky scream. Then it spreads its wings and flies away to hunt mice or other animals. Indian childen often hide when they hear these hoots and screams, for owls are supposed to be ghosts of warriors that died long ago. No Indian likes to be out in the mountains when those "ghosts" begin to call!

Horned owls seem to like campgrounds and so do some nutcrackers, which also are called Clarke crows. They are large gray birds with black-and-white wings and tails. They walk on the ground like crows and often pick up bits of food that were dropped or thrown away by campers.

The best place to see nutcrackers, however, is in the Hudsonian Zone. There they nest in the stunted evergreens long before most of us come to the mountains. The young birds are fed on pine seeds which the parents get from cones. When summer comes, the nutcrackers eat berries, grubs, grasshoppers, beetles, and several other things. They often perch on treetops and call *Karr-r-rr, karr-rr!* in hoarse voices. They can go from one life zone to another in a hurry, for they often fly from high ledges and swoop down into valleys. There they alight on the tops of trees, teetering till they get their balance.

Ravens look like huge black crows with thick beaks. They build their nests in trees or on cliffs that are much too steep for us to climb. But we often see grown-up

Horned Owl

Rocky Mountain
Jay

Steller Jay

Nutcracker

ravens plainly as they eat dead animals near the highway. They soar like hawks or vultures when they look for food, and croak instead of cawing as crows do. You can tell a raven by its croaking and soaring, even when it is so far away that you cannot see its beak.

While we watch ravens soar above a glacier a bird on the ground says *Cluck-uk-uk* in a low, soft voice. This is the ptarmigan, whose name is pronounced without the *p*. It looks a bit like a large quail with feathers on its legs and feet. Yet we have to watch closely to see it at all, for its yellowish-brown and gray feathers make it resemble the plants and stones that cover the ground. Just now only its wings and tail are white. When winter comes it will grow a new coat of feathers that will be as white as snow.

Mother ptarmigans build their nests on the ground, high up in the Hudsonian or Arctic-Alpine zones. Here they lay ten to sixteen buff eggs that are spotted with brown and black. When the eggs hatch, each mother bird takes her little ones to a place where they can drink. Soon they eat pollen from dryad flowers; then they begin to pick buds and catch flies or other insects.

At night the mother covers her chicks with her wings; in the daytime she keeps watch for danger. When she gives a warning cluck the babies "freeze," which means that they crouch down on the ground and keep as still as stones. They also look like stones that are covered with gray and brown lichens.

BIRDS IN FOUR LIFE ZONES

The whole ptarmigan family "freezes" while a golden eagle soars above the mountain side. This big bird is almost three feet long; when it spreads its wings, they are more than six feet wide. Its neck and legs are yellowish brown, and it has feathers all the way to its toes. Those feathers show that it isn't a young bald eagle, whose lower legs are bare.

Some golden eagles build big nests on top of high trees a few hundred feet above our campground. Others use ledges on high cliffs, where mountain goats sometimes climb. They hunt marmots, grouse, and ground squirrels, but sometimes they catch young deer. If food becomes scarce, golden eagles will fly to the foothills or plains and bring back jack rabbits for their young ones to eat. Ranchmen complain that they kill lambs, but they do so only when other food is very hard to find.

At last we come to the Arctic-Alpine Zone, where carpet pinks and dryads grow near white snowbanks. For a while we see no birds at all. Then a grayish-brown

Raven

Golden Eagle

pipit flies down and hops about on the snow. It is picking up seeds that were dropped by winds which brought them from lower places. Other pipits come to hunt dead insects.

They chirp happily, *Chip-chee, cheep!* They also nod their heads and bob their tails as they go from one place to another, looking for things to eat. Then they fly away, till at last they disappear in the air above a snowy peak.

CHAPTER XV

What to See and Where to Find It

A S WE SAID in Chapter I, there are mountains in both the East and the West, and from South America to Alaska. Most of us, however, are much too busy to visit all these ranges and peaks. We must choose those that are not too far from home and not too hard to reach. We also want them to be specially fine, with the very best of everything that tells the story of mountains.

Luckily, millions of other people want just about what we do. To help them and us, nations have set aside their most beautiful highlands as national parks, forests, and preserves known as monuments. These scenic regions can be reached by railways and good paved roads. Most of them have camps or hotels where we may stay and trails on which we may ride or hike. They make it easy for us to see the mountains and enjoy them on our vacation trips.

Which of these regions shall we choose to visit? Some

people don't bother to choose; they just go to one park or forest after the other until it is time to come home. They travel so fast that they see very little, and may not even have a good time.

Other travelers do not hurry. They decide exactly what they want to see and go to the right places to find it. Such people will visit volcanoes on one trip, blister mountains on another, and so on year after year. Still others select the mountains in one special part of the country, or those along one or two special highways. These people also do not hurry, but try to see as much as they can in every region they visit.

One of these plans is as good as the other; follow the one you like. But, no matter which plan you prefer, you will want to know what can be seen in the various mountain wonderlands. Chapters in this book will answer many of your questions, and so will the illustrations. As a further help, here is a list of mountain parks, monuments, and forests in both Canada and the United States. It is not complete, but it does mention the best ones and tells some of the things you will see when you visit them.

The Black Hills, in southwestern South Dakota, are part national forest, part state park, and part privately owned land. Instead of being hills, they are blister mountains of granite in the midst of rolling plains. Part of the cover still is preserved, and there are hogbacks of limestone and sandstone. The granite contains a great deal of pegmatite and has been weathered into marvelous pinnacles. North and west of the Hills are several laccoliths, including Green Mountain.

Devil's Tower, in eastern Wyoming, is a national monument. The tower consists of porphyry that filled the neck of a volcano which was worn away ages ago. As the rock hardened it broke into curved columns that are hundreds of feet in height.

Rocky Mountain National Park, in Colorado, often is known as Estes Park. It is a region of granite batholiths that were worn into a rolling plain and then pushed upward. Frost, streams, and glaciers cut the uplifted plain into mountains with U-shaped canyons and cirques. One of the finest cirques is near the Trail Ridge Road; it contains Iceberg Lake. There are limber pines and other trees, and many flowers. Beaver dams lie near the highway, and herds of elk may be seen. The mountains are so much higher than the country around them that rain falls almost every day. Start out early and don't hurry back to camp if you want to take pictures. And by the way—why not get some shots of a real mountain storm?

The Big Horn Mountains, in Wyoming, also are an uplifted batholith whose cover is partly preserved. You'll see it in Tensleep or Shell Canyon and will notice how the beds are tilted. If you take color pictures, go to the mouth of Shell Canyon late in the afternoon. The colors and tilted rocks are as fine as anything you'll find in the West!

Yosemite National Park, in California, contains the most scenic part of the Sierra Nevada, which is described in Chapter VIII. The granite batholith is gray; it has been worn into cliffs, domes, and deep valleys. Glaciers have left many hanging valleys with fine waterfalls. The forests contain bigtrees, sugar pines, and many other species. Black bears and Columbia blacktail deer are common in the campgrounds. King's Canyon National Park, south of the Yosemite, is rather like it but much more wild.

Sequoia National Park also is in the Sierra Nevada. It contains the finest groves of bigtrees, as well as Mount Whitney, which is the highest peak in the United States —if we leave out Alaska.

Mount Rainier National Park, in western Washington, is named for its huge, dead volcano. It should be even more famous for its many large glaciers, which are easily seen. Forests are large and thick, and wild flowers are abundant. Sports include riding, climbing, and skiing.

Mount Hood, in northwestern Oregon, and Mount Shasta, in northern California, are famous dead volcanoes in national forests. You can drive quite close to Mount Hood, but Shasta is farther from good roads than it seems.

WHAT TO SEE AND WHERE TO FIND IT

Lassen Volcanic National Park also is in northern California, near the southern end of the Cascades. It is the best place to see plug domes made by very stiff lava. It also has fine block lava flows, a cinder cone, and forests of ponderosa and Jeffrey pines. At greater heights we find mountain hemlocks. Trees are just beginning to grow upon the land covered by mud flows during the eruptions of 1915.

There is some ropy lava near the tunnels north of Lassen Park. But the finest place to see such flows is the Craters of the Moon National Monument, in southeastern Idaho. Though these flows are at least six hundred years old, they glisten as if they had just hardened. The monument also contains some fine cinder cones. Near-by mountains are made of tilted rocks and resemble ranges in the desert near Great Salt Lake.

Crater Lake National Park, in southwestern Oregon, contains the remains of a volcano that exploded and then collapsed. The result was a huge bowl, now filled by a deep blue lake. There are forests of ponderosa pines, mountain hemlocks, and other trees. Life zones show plainly.

Yellowstone National Park, in northwestern Wyoming, is famous for its hot springs, geysers, and wild animals. It also has some old volcanoes, but most of the park is a lava plateau. Visitors who come from Cody cross the Absaroka Mountains, which are mostly lava and agglomerate. The road from Red Lodge, Montana, passes many mountain lakes and crosses alpine meadows.

Grand Teton National Park, south of the Yellowstone, is not at all like it. The steep mountains and deep, U-shaped canyons have been worn from a block of metamorphic rocks that was broken and tilted upward. The small glaciers that remain are rather hard to reach, but trails through the valleys are wide and easy. Those who don't want to hike may go boating on pleasant lakes.

Death Valley National Monument, in southeastern California, contains block mountains and the lowest land in North America. It is a fine place to see the desert valleys and mountains described in Chapter VIII, but is much too hot for summer visits. Joshua Tree National Monument, also in southern California, contains weathered mountains of granite and interesting desert plants.

Olympic National Park, in northwestern Washington, is about as different from Death Valley as any region can be. It has glaciers, fogs, and a great deal of snow. Forests of Douglas firs are so thick that they suggest tropical woodlands. There are many wild animals, including the big, dark Roosevelt elk. This animal also can be seen at Prairie Creek State Park, in the redwoods of northern California.

Glacier National Park, in northwestern Montana, has about sixty small glaciers and many deep U-shaped valleys. It also is the best place to see a great thrust fault, which is described in Chapter V. The ancient marine rocks are brightly colored and contain many ripple marks, mud cracks, and other structures. Life zones show plainly on the steep mountains, and limber pines fit themselves to different surroundings. The frontispiece shows one of the Park's largest and most interesting lakes.

Waterton Lakes Park, in southern Alberta, is much like Glacier but not so large. The most famous Canadian parks are farther north. Banff Park, in Alberta, has ranges of mountains that were pushed upward along thrust faults. There are large glaciers and some fine horn peaks. Moose are common and grizzly bears may be seen in some valleys.

Jasper Park also is in Alberta; a good road connects it with Banff. This road passes large ice fields and glaciers.

Yoho Park, in British Columbia, contains the fossil quarry described in Chapter VI. It also has glaciers, steep mountains, and U-shaped valleys. Life zones show plainly along some trails, and there is one very high falls that comes from a hanging valley.

Dinosaur National Monument is partly in northwestern Colorado and partly in Utah. It is famous for its fossil bones, but it should be just as famous for its canyons, its arched rocks with bright colors, and its steep hogbacks. If you take color photographs, you will enjoy it almost as much as Glacier Park.

Shenandoah National Park, in Virginia, gives visitors a fine idea of the folded and worn mountains in the

Appalachians. There are thrust faults here, too, but soil and woods hide them.

Great Smokies National Park is partly in North Carolina and partly in Tennessee. Its rocks are bent and faulted, and have been worn so much that they seldom form steep cliffs. The thick forests contain one hundred and forty kinds of trees, of which one hundred and twenty-nine are native. There are many meadows, or "balds," where no trees grow, though the ground is covered with grass. No one knows why trees do not grow on these "bald" places.

This brings us to the end of our list. Good luck when you use it as a guide on visits to America's mountains!

Index

Index

This index gives the pronunciation of technical terms and some names. Ordinary numbers refer to pages, but those in heavy type indicate photographs which face those pages.

INDEX

INDEX

INDEX

INDEX

INDEX

Thimbleberry, 118, 119.
Thrust fault, 50, 52.
Tilted Mountain, Banff Park, 69.
Tilted rocks, **11**.
Transition Zone, 114.
Trilobite (try' lo bite), 59, **65**.
Trout, 133, 134.
Tuff, 34.

Upper Klamath (clam'ath) Lake, Ore., 73, **77**, 80.

Valley glaciers, 85.
Valleys, glaciated, 96.
  hanging, **10**, 96.
Volcanic bombs, 35.
Volcanic dust, 34.
Volcanic glass, 33.
Volcanoes, 23, 26, **29**, **36**, 85.
Vulcano, Italy, 23.

Wapiti, 124.
Wasatch Mountains, 78, 80.

Waterton Lakes Park, Alberta, 151.
Weathering, 67, **84**.
Western hemlock, 103, 108.
Western larch, 103, 109.
Western white pine, 104, 107.
Western yellow pine, 104, **108**.
Whistler, **133**.
White dryad, 110, **116**, 121.
White fir, 106, 107.
Wild geranium, 118, 119.
Willows, **116**, 120.

Yarrow, 115.
Yellow-haired porcupine, 131, **132**.
Yellowstone Nat. Park, Wyo., 149.
Yoho Park, British Columbia, 151.
Yosemite Falls, Calif., 96.
Yosemite Nat. Park, **68**, 96, 148.

Zones, life, 112.